Cognitive Behavioral Therapy (CBT) for Misophonia

By Shaylynn Hayes-Raymond

Misophonia International

COGNITIVE BEHAVIORAL THERAPY (CBT) FOR
MISOPHONIA © 2025

Published by Misophonia International

Distributed by Imperceptions Press

Cover art and print/eBook design
by Imperceptions Press

Edited by Harrison Porter

Print ISBN: 978-1-990467-45-5

Hardcover ISBN: 978-1-990467-47-9

Ebook ISBN: 978-1-990467-46-2

Table of Contents

Introduction

The purpose of this book is for clinicians helping
persons with misophonia or for persons with misophonia to
learn how to cope with the condition from a CBT
perspective. This book is an introduction and outline to
CBT-MISO, a CBT program for misophonia which is
proposed by this author, Shaylynn Hayes-Raymond. This
approach to CBT has several adaptions, including less
emphasis on behavioral experiments and the omission of
exposure therapy. While psychoeducation is extremely
important for newer conditions like misophonia, this will
not be covered heavily in this text as it has already been
covered by the author extensively in her prior work,
Misophonia Matters, which provided an overview of
misophonia. However, necessary psychoeducation is
provided where its absence would lead to confusion during
the CBT-MISO approach outlined. If you are new to the
condition entirely, it may be useful to start with *Misophonia
Matters* before diving into this work. For the sake of length,
this book will focus more on practical coping tips for
misophonia from a cognitive behavioral therapy perspective.
This book includes worksheets, prompts, and tools that may
be used by individuals or clinicians. The author of this book
grants permission to all clinicians using this book to reprint
and copy worksheets for the sake of clinical use in their own

practice—but not for redistribution through their own website or media. Some parts of *Misophonia Matters* have been repeated in this book where necessary to integrate CBT-MISO and *Misophonia Matters*.

About This Book

In my prior book *Misophonia Matters,* I strongly encourage clinicians and those suffering with misophonia to understand that advocacy and communication are paramount for coping with misophonia and adapting to a world that does not suit the needs of the individual. Rather than a replacement for, or a different perspective from, *Misophonia Matters*, this book is meant to provide a more in-depth offering of worksheets, skills, and perspectives for part 5 of *Misophonia Matters* criteria which are "Cognitive and Psychological Strategies". This book is meant to be used as part of the *Misophonia Matters* perspective, but it also provides an exclusive treatment plan from the CBT perspective, and thus CBT-MISO can be used in conjunction with Misophonia Matters or on its own. It would be useful to become familiar with my prior works before working through this book yourself or with clients. While it is not necessary to read the prior book, it is necessary to understand that this book merely provides an in-depth perspective on one part out of five. The five parts of the *Misophonia Matters* approach are as follows:

Part One: Psychoeducation
Part Two: Advocacy and Explaining
Part Three: Accommodations and Negotiations
Part Four: Sensory-Based Strategies
Part Five: Cognitive and Psychological Strategies

It is worth noting that part five can include far more coping skills from a psychological perspective than just CBT—such as narrative, Gestalt, psychodynamic, and other perspectives. For the sake of brevity, this book will focus exclusively on CBT which has been shown in research to be beneficial for misophonia (Schröder, 2017; Jager, 2021). However, this is not to say that I am promoting only CBT as a psychological strategy for misophonia, as I often employ numerous eclectic strategies in my own clinical practice and in my day-to-day life with misophonia.

While all five steps are important to coping with misophonia, this particular text assumes you are already acquainted with misophonia and are looking for a more practical deep dive into specific skills that can be used in clinical counselling or on your own as a self-help tool. If you do not fully understand misophonia or feel lost, I highly suggest reading my prior book *Misophonia Matters* or exploring the work of Dr. Jennifer Jo Brout who provides thorough and easily digestible explanations of misophonia.

Throughout this book, you will find worksheets and examples for a CBT-based approach to misophonia. In some cases, there are numerous worksheets on a similar topic without additional introductory text. These worksheets can be used by clinicians in their practice or by individuals with misophonia. The final section of this book includes all worksheets on their own in an easy to copy format.

Cognitive Behavioral Therapy (CBT) for Misophonia

Who am I?

My name is Shaylynn Hayes-Raymond and I am a counsellor in New Brunswick, Canada. I have been an advocate for misophonia since learning about the condition in 2014, and I published my first book on the subject, *Full of Sound and Fury: Living with Misophonia,* in 2015. My interest in misophonia and learning more about it came to fruition through personal experience. Almost suddenly at age 19 I began to react to the world around me differently, whereby I was confused and frustrated by the tumultuous fight-flight-freeze experience I had when faced with otherwise normal stimuli such as legs shaking, whistling, tapping, and pens clicking. I did not know it at the time, but I would soon find out that I was suffering from something called *misophonia*. After learning about the condition, as well as the lack of research and awareness on the subject, I became dedicated to the cause. In the early years it was about self-preservation, as I needed to be trying my best to advocate for misophonia because the condition was impacting my life to an enormous degree. Advocacy was my coping method.

After graduating with a Bachelor of Arts in Political Science, I undertook my Master of Arts in Counselling Psychology. I was driven to complete this degree and become a counsellor because I wanted to help persons with misophonia like myself. I will say that several professors throughout my degree mentioned that I was hyper-focused on misophonia. Some believed I should be less focused on one condition, but at my core, misophonia was the *reason* why I was there, and was the reason why I felt so passionate about undertaking a career in the counselling profession. Today I am the Director of The International Misophonia Foundation, run a private practice for therapy, and offer coaching coping sessions worldwide for persons with misophonia. I am also passionate about providing education and resources to clinicians interested in supporting those with misophonia. While this book draws from cognitive behavioral therapy, my core passion is about coping with misophonia.

Much of my work involves talking to people with misophonia and seeing what helps them, assessing my own coping strategies, and taking a compassionate approach which understands that persons with misophonia are not simply lacking control of their emotions and behaviors, but are instead subject to a very real, very disorienting, physiological response.

What does CBT for Misophonia Entail?

Cognitive Behavioral Therapy (CBT) for misophonia involves surrounding the moment of misophonia—not the trigger itself, and learning how to adapt to and live with the complex emotions that come from a fight-flight-freeze response to auditory (or visual) stimuli. CBT for misophonia should in my opinion not include exposure therapy, as this has been noted by persons with misophonia to be highly uncomfortable. This is not to say that CBT cannot be helpful for misophonia, but that a phobia or OCD-based treatment plan for misophonia is not appropriate for those suffering with misophonia. Instead, CBT for misophonia should revolve around what the person with misophonia *can* control instead of alleviating the trigger entirely. CBT-MISO is specifically adapted to use the parts of CBT that can help an individual deal with the emotional and behavioral impact of misophonia outside of the precipitatory moment of fight-flight-freeze.

While evidence for any treatment method for misophonia is still in its infancy, a 2021 randomized clinical trial determined that "the CBT group had an observed clinical improvement in 37% compared to 0% in the waiting list group" (Jager et al., 2021). Jager went on to note that these changes were still maintained at one-year follow-up appointments. This provides peer-reviewed evidence that CBT has some benefit for misophonia by offering an improvement over the control group which received no intervention and maintained the same level of impairment on the scale used for the study.

The Cycle of Misophonia

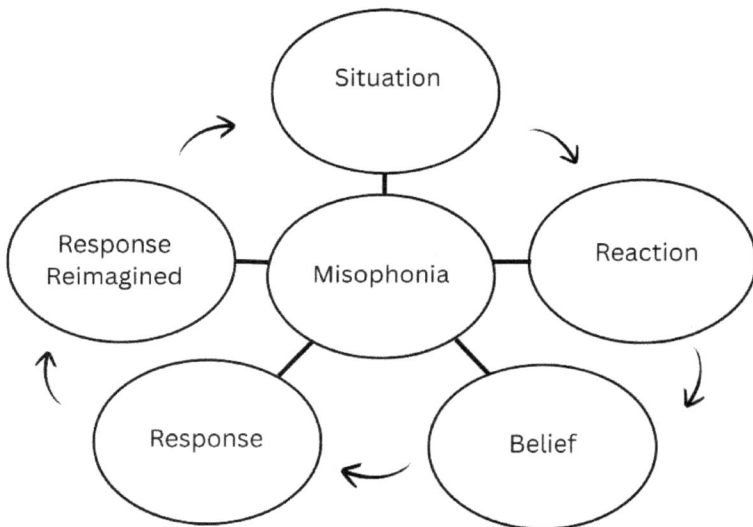

The cognitive model introduced in this book is meant to adapt common CBT principles with other techniques for coping with misophonia, and thus I have labeled this approach CBT-MISO. The above diagram shows misophonia as the central issue, with each cognitive and behavioral stage presented in a circular pattern. Misophonia is *central* rather than the main situation/reaction to highlight the neurophysiological nature of misophonia which is external to psychological cognition and behavior.

Since cognitive behavioral therapy is a type of therapy modality, and not only *one* specific therapy, there are variabilities that can be used to cope. Some people may prefer one exercise, where others will be drawn to a different one. The key to coping with a disorder like misophonia is not to try and fit a square peg into a round hole, but rather to discover what is appropriate for each person's needs. No exercise in this book is meant to be *one size fits all,* but instead should be taken as a starter point and a guide for coping with misophonia. Current misophonia research has shown CBT to be beneficial for coping (Schröder, 2017; Jager, 2021), but even still, I want to caution clinicians and persons with misophonia that *coping* will look different for each individual. There is no right or wrong way to cope with misophonia, and it is not a personal failure if an exercise does not resonate with an individual. Instead, these exercises should be used as jumping off points and ideas rather than prescriptive measures.

Exposure Therapy and Misophonia

Exposure and Response Prevention (ERP) is often used and considered a gold-standard for treatment of disorders involving panic and anxiety such as Obsessive Compulsive Disorder (OCD). Current misophonia literature points out that misophonia is likely a neurophysiological disorder with a motor-basis, fight-flight-freeze response, and sensory dysregulation. With this knowledge in mind, exposure therapy is an irresponsible therapy choice for persons with misophonia.

Misophonia, a condition characterized by intense emotional and physiological reactions to specific sounds, has often been misunderstood by both healthcare professionals and researchers. While the understanding of misophonia continues to grow, certain treatments, particularly exposure therapy, have consistently proven ineffective and even detrimental for those affected. As I have often noted, if exposure therapy were a viable solution for misophonia, individuals would already be cured. Unlike phobias, exposure to misophonia triggers is typically a daily occurrence for most people, and individuals often cannot completely avoid or isolate themselves from these sounds. Everyday noises such as sneezing, coughing, chewing, or birds chirping can cause significant distress to someone with misophonia.

Emerging research clearly illustrates why exposure therapy falls short as a treatment method for misophonia. Online communities, such as the /r/misophonia subreddit and various private Facebook groups and support forums, are filled with personal accounts from members who report that exposure therapy exacerbated their symptoms. These communities consistently express concern over this "treatment" method, highlighting its lack of supporting evidence and potential to worsen the condition.

Research by Kumar et al. (2017) indicates that misophonia involves atypical neural connections between the auditory cortex and brain regions responsible for emotional regulation, such as the anterior insular cortex (AIC). This suggests that misophonia is not a fear-based or learned response, but rather a deeply ingrained neurophysiological condition. Unlike phobias, which exposure therapy aims to alleviate by reducing fear, misophonia triggers an instinctive response that bypasses conventional cognitive processing (Kumar et al., 2017).

A 2018 literature review by Dr. Jennifer Jo Brout and her colleagues emphasizes the importance of psychoeducation and sensory-informed approaches over traditional therapeutic methods. Small-scale studies promoting exposure therapy often overlook participant biases, including the placebo effect and cognitive dissonance. Many participants initially report satisfaction due to feeling validated by clinicians, rather than from the actual efficacy of the therapy. This phenomenon can skew research outcomes and perpetuate the misconception that exposure therapy is effective (Brout, 2018).

Recent studies further suggest that misophonia is linked to hyperconnectivity in brain networks responsible for integrating sensory and emotional information (Kumar, 2017; Neacsiu, 2022). This helps explain why repeated exposure does not lead to habituation, but instead intensifies the distress caused by triggers.

Exposure therapy is based on the principle of desensitization, which assumes that repeated exposure to a feared stimulus reduces its emotional intensity over time. However, misophonia is not a phobia; it is not rooted in fear or avoidance. The emotional response to triggers is involuntary and neurologically embedded, rendering exposure ineffective.

Numerous individuals with misophonia have reported that exposure therapy not only failed to alleviate their symptoms but also caused additional harm, including heightened anxiety, increased avoidance behaviors, and even symptoms typical of PTSD. In surveys I conducted with over 300 individuals with misophonia, many participants stated they felt worse after exposure therapy, often citing a lack of follow-up and acknowledgment of their experiences.

Power imbalances in research also play a role. Participants in studies may feel compelled to report positive outcomes, even if the treatment was ineffective. Numerous individuals have shared in social media groups and support forums that they did not want to disappoint clinicians or researchers, leading to skewed results. (I have not linked to these sources to protect the privacy of these communities.) This dynamic undermines the validity of exposure therapy studies and raises ethical concerns.

Evidence suggests that more effective approaches for misophonia include psychoeducation, which helps individuals understand the neurological and emotional mechanisms underlying misophonia. Sensory accommodations are also beneficial, utilizing tools such as sound-dampening devices, noise-canceling headphones, or modifying environments to reduce exposure to triggers. Emotion regulation techniques, such as mindfulness practices, relaxation exercises, and strategies to manage physiological arousal, can also be helpful. While not a cure for misophonia, Cognitive Behavioral Therapy (CBT) can address secondary issues that arise from the condition, such as anxiety or social isolation.

Clinicians and researchers must acknowledge the distinct neurological and emotional profile of misophonia and move away from harmful practices such as exposure therapy. It is crucial to listen to those with relevant personal experiences to develop ethical and effective interventions. As someone living with misophonia, I can attest to the distress this condition causes, and the harm inflicted by misguided treatments. It is time for the field to advance with approaches founded on compassion, scientific evidence, and respect for individual experiences.

By prioritizing research-backed methods and rejecting harmful interventions, we can pave the way for a future where individuals with misophonia receive genuine support, rather than being retraumatized in therapy. Various misophonia resources are available to help individuals cope with the condition.

Cognitive Behavioral Therapy (CBT) for Misophonia

The Fallible Clinician

I want to be very clear to those reading this book—whether you are a clinician or a person with misophonia—that *treatment* for misophonia is not meant to be a cure that alleviates misophonia entirely. Research is still ongoing and there is no method of alleviating misophonia entirely. For the purpose of this text, the word *treatment* refers to psychological and sensory regulation-based interventions to help alleviate the suffering of those with misophonia, and not to promise a miracle. I often refer to coping with misophonia as *management* or *coping skills* to help differentiate these exercises and interventions from ones which have been shown in research to completely mitigate a disorder or illness. Rather, in this book you will find ways to help sufferers of misophonia to cope with the reality of living with the condition day to day.

With that said, I am hopeful that misophonia research will continue to expand, and in the future, we may see more rigorous treatments which include a more in-depth mitigation of the condition. While we are not there yet, I am hopeful that we will eventually see more robust ways to cope with and manage misophonia. If you are interested in learning more about advocacy, education, and research on misophonia you can visit the website for The International Misophonia Foundation: www.misophoniafoundation.com.

Through my ten years of advocacy and my last few years as a clinician, I have come to have multiple perspectives on clinicians who are *treating* misophonia. In many cases, clinicians are just as confused as their clients with misophonia and are often working on whatever information or lens is most readily available. I will *never* be okay with clinicians throwing whatever they can at the wall and seeing what sticks—but, I must say that I have more empathy for practitioners who have come into contact with persons with misophonia and tried to help them.

In some cases, these clinicians have employed an OCD perspective which considers misophonia like a phobia. The problem is that misophonia is not a cognitive reaction at its onset, and thus the distress is the aftermath of a physiological response. No amount of exposure will teach the brain not to have any physiological response in these circumstances, and while cognitive skills are useful, exposure therapy is not.

With that said, as of 2025, misophonia is not in the DSM-5 or ICD. For all intents and purposes misophonia exists everywhere but on paper. Even the most well-meaning clinician may not have access to information to adequately help those with misophonia. I do believe these clinicians are well-meaning and perhaps suffering from burnout and an inability to take courses and trainings or even find them in the first place for such a new condition. Clinical counselling is a fallible profession and while many of us try our hardest to provide the utmost care possible, at the end of the day we only have so many resources and misophonia is not currently commonly taught in graduate classes or in any part of standard psychological trainings.

This is not to say that an individual should stay with a practitioner who does not understand misophonia or who provides exposure therapy against the protestations of their clients. Instead, this suggests that clients have an opportunity to bridge the gap and provide educational materials for clinicians to access. For example, clinicians could be encouraged to take a clinician class through the International Misophonia Foundation.

A Note on Assessment

While there are some misophonia assessments in existence, I have not mentioned any particular form of assessment since misophonia is not yet in a diagnostic manual. It is my profound hope that as editions of this book are updated, we will eventually see a more thorough diagnostic standard for misophonia. In the meantime, clinicians and persons with misophonia can use the limited measures which exist if they prefer to. It is my belief that the assessment for misophonia is less important since most persons struggling with such a new phenomenon would not seek out help if they did not have the symptoms that commonly characterize misophonia.

The following assessments may be useful for misophonia, but the author of this work offers them as-is and does not support any particular measure over another:

- **Amsterdam Misophonia Scale (A-MISO-S):** This is one of the more commonly cited scales, adapted from measures used for obsessive-compulsive disorder.
- **Misophonia Assessment Questionnaire (MAQ):** This questionnaire assesses various aspects of misophonia, including emotional and physical responses, as well as impacts on daily life.
- **Misophonia Activation Scale (MAS-1):** Developed by Misophonia-uk.org, this scale aims to evaluate the severity of misophonia on a 1-10 scale.

- **Misophonia Severity Scale (MSS):** Another tool designed to gauge the intensity of misophonic reactions.
- **Berlin Misophonia Questionnaire (BMQ):** This questionnaire also contributes to the assessment landscape for misophonia.
- **MisoQuest:** This is a validated questionnaire used to assess misophonia symptoms and impact.
- **Duke Misophonia Questionnaire (DMQ) / Duke Misophonia Interview (DMI):** These instruments, particularly the DMI, are semi-structured clinical interviews designed to assess an individual's misophonia experience.

10 Week Misophonia CBT Plan (CBT-MISO)

This book is written with a 10-week cognitive behavioral therapy plan for misophonia in mind. It is designed to either be used in a therapist-client capacity or as a self-help book. For therapists, 10 sessions are considered the necessary amount to dedicate to the full book—for self-help readers, this translates to 1-2 hour(s) per week for 10 weeks. For at home readers, it is not recommended to skip ahead and do exercises in quick succession. This program is meant to be done in a way that allows for significant understanding of each section before moving on to the next.

To help differentiate CBT for misophonia from other forms of CBT, I will be calling this particular program CBT-MISO. The purpose of this volume is to provide an overview and preliminary understanding of CBT for misophonia from a neurophysiological, sensory, and emotional basis.

Therapists offering this CBT-MISO program for misophonia may also be interested in reading *Misophonia Matters* which provides further worksheets and tools on accommodations, negotiations, sensory diets, and more. While this book has been laid out in a way that is conducive to the following 10-week program, it can also be adapted to longer or shorter sessions, or as a do-it-yourself format where you go at your own pace.

10 Week Misophonia CBT Program Overview

1. **Understanding Misophonia (Psychoeducation)**: This section focuses on the basics of misophonia and learning about the condition from current literature.

2. **Goal setting:** While this part of the book does not include lengthy text, it is imperative to spend enough time on the exercise so that persons with misophonia can be clear in their goals for coping with misophonia.

3. **Beliefs and values:** This section focuses on determining beliefs and values surrounding misophonia.

4. **The impact of misophonia:** This section focuses on the impact misophonia has on the lives of those who suffer from the condition, as well as the precipitating moments of misophonia.

5. **Automatic thoughts/patterns:** This section focuses on the automatic thoughts that come with misophonia and cognitive tools for managing these thoughts.

6. **Misophonia coping skills**: This section focuses on coping skills for misophonia as well as tools and accommodations for alleviating distress. The final part of this section focuses on ensuring that coping skills are

used. Each sub-section is broken down into its own week to ensure ample focus on the topic.

6. Adaptive tools.

7. Physiological.

8. Accommodations.

9. Planning around misophonia.

10. Sustaining Progress: This section includes worksheets on sustaining progress and celebrating successes that were achieved throughout this program.

Cognitive Behavioral Therapy (CBT) for Misophonia

Misophonia in a CBT Framework

CBT is meant to take less time than traditional psychotherapy and talk therapy. With that in mind, most CBT programs aim to initiate change in the individual within a set number of sessions. These sessions can be week to week, bi-weekly, or in any structure that is both psychologically and financially feasible for the individual receiving CBT. In the CBT-MISO program in this book, I discuss an approach that is meant to be done in 10 sessions that are each one hour. Some individuals may require more sessions in different areas, and that is for the clinician or individual to decide.

In *Cognitive Behavioral Therapy in 7 Weeks* Gilligan (2016) lays out a 7-week plan for CBT which includes the following weekly goals for CBT: 1. Setting goals, 2. Values, 3. Identifying thought patterns, 4. Breaking negative thought patterns, 5. Time and task management, 6. Facing fears, and 7. Putting it all together.

Based on principles from Cognitive Behavioral Therapy and Acceptance and Commitment Therapy, the following table outlines how core beliefs, intermediate beliefs, thought patterns, and values interact in conditions like misophonia. This model is based on the foundational cognitive hierarchy developed by Judith Beck (2011), which outlines how deep beliefs influence automatic thoughts and emotional responses. For the purposes of this book, I have expanded the model to include values, which guide purposeful action, and thought patterns (also known as cognitive distortions), based on the work of Gillihan (2016) which help identify recurring styles of unhelpful thinking. I have also removed "behaviors and reactions" from this model to better align with a physiological approach to misophonia and have instead listed "misophonia coping skills" in its place.

CBT-MISO Hierarchy of Cognition

Hierarchy Level	Corresponding Chapter	Description	Example in Misophonia
1. Core Beliefs	Beliefs and Values	Deep, global beliefs about self or the world.	"I'm not safe." / "People don't care."
2. Intermediate Beliefs	(Covered within *Beliefs and Values*)	Rules and assumptions from core beliefs.	"They should stop." / "I'll lose control."
3. Values	(Covered within *Beliefs and Values*)	What truly matters to you.	"I value calm and emotional control."
4. The Impact of Misophonia	The Impact of Misophonia	Physiological and sensory reactions to a trigger.	Sudden jolt, increased heart rate, sensory overload.
5. Automatic Thoughts	Automatic Thoughts and Their Patterns	Quick thoughts or urges after a trigger.	"They're doing it to annoy me."
6. Thought Patterns	(Covered within *Automatic Thoughts and Their Patterns*)	Recurring styles of thinking.	Exaggerated: "This will ruin my day." Intent Attributing: "They're doing it on purpose."
7. Coping Skills	Misophonia Coping Skills	The emotional and behavioral results.	Anxiety, anger, frustration, avoidance.

Cognitive Behavioral Therapy (CBT) for Misophonia

Identifying Goals for Coping with Misophonia

Whether you are a clinician working with a client with misophonia, a person with misophonia, or a parent looking for coping skills for your child, it is important to identify goals for coping with misophonia. These goals should not be chosen and led by a clinician or parent but rather should be identified by the client as their personal goals for coping with misophonia. If your client or child is resistant, it can be helpful to make suggestions based on observed behavior, but do not impose these goals. It is also important that goals for coping with misophonia reflect on the core beliefs and values of the individual—not the other parties involved. If you have strong views one way or another about *how one should cope* it may be necessary to allow the client or child to reflect on these goals on their own in a private journal before sharing. The following are example goals for coping with misophonia. I have only shared three examples as it is best to keep goals manageable in the beginning. Later on, in sessions more goals may arise as coping skills are developed.

Goals for Coping with Misophonia

It is important for clinicians and persons with misophonia to understand that *misophonia is not a psychological phenomenon*, but rather has a neurological brain basis (Kumar, 2017), whereby the physiological part of the equation must be considered paramount when developing goals for misophonia. Goals should be realistic and highlight ways in which thoughts and perceptions of misophonia *can change* rather than engaging in wishful thinking. It is not reasonable at this time to have goals such as "Have misophonia go away completely" or "Never be bothered by sounds". Goal setting should not revolve around exposure therapy or desensitizing persons with misophonia as this increases distress levels and can lead to worse cognitive distortions (e.g. I will never feel better, this is terrible; I cannot be fixed, I am broken, etc.).

Like any physical ailment or condition—persons with misophonia can learn to cope in the moments surrounding the misophonic trigger but cannot change the reality of the fight-flight-freeze response to stimuli. For example, it would be inappropriate to tell a person permanently in a wheelchair that they can have the goal to "walk again completely" unless that is medically possible. At this time, there is no indication of a treatment that can permanently alleviate symptoms of misophonia (Brout, 2018; Swedo, 2022).

Worksheet: Goals for Coping with Misophonia

Instructions: List three personal goals for managing your misophonia.

1. _____

2. _____

3. _____

Cognitive Behavioral Therapy (CBT) for Misophonia

Example: Goals for Coping with Misophonia

Instructions: List three personal goals for managing your misophonia.

1. *Be able to stay in uncomfortable situations.*
2. *Enjoy moments not triggered without worrying.*
3. *Not avoid situations in case there are triggers.*

Cognitive Behavioral Therapy (CBT) for Misophonia

Section 1: Understanding Misophonia

Misophonia is a highly debated topic. While some characterize it as a psychiatric condition involving an overreaction to stimuli, I view it differently. To me, misophonia represents an atypical neurological processing of auditory and visual information (Kumar et al., 2017). Despite ongoing debate, this disorder profoundly impacts individuals' lives, and yet a universally accepted definition remains elusive. From a personal standpoint, misophonia has been life-altering. It transforms everyday existence into a constant negotiation of triggers and potential triggers. The scientific discussions surrounding its nature do not diminish the very real suffering and pain it inflicts upon those who experience it. Scientifically, I consider misophonia to constitute a neurophysiological disorder where otherwise non-aversive stimuli provoke a fight-flight-freeze response (Brout et al., 2018). However, this scientific explanation often falls short in conveying the daily challenges faced by individuals with misophonia. As researchers engage in academic discussions about affected brain regions and conduct treatment studies yielding only marginal results, those living with misophonia continue to grapple with a condition they perceive as a personal hell. Misophonia research is relatively new within the fields of neuroscience and psychology. The term itself was coined in 2001 by audiologists Drs. Jastreboff and Jastreboff who observed distinct differences among patients with tinnitus, hyperacusis, and misophonia (Jastreboff and Jastreboff, 2001). A vibrant online culture has emerged around misophonia, with support groups and websites dedicated to assisting researchers and providing a platform for individuals to share their experiences. These communities, including social media groups and non-profit organizations, advocate for "misophones" and are outspoken about the value of research and the stigma associated with the disorder (Misophonia International, n.d.). Many with misophonia express frustration with exposure therapy, believing that if it were effective, they would already be cured given the unavoidable nature of common sensory stimuli like coughing, chewing, whistling, and pen tapping. Although still in its early stages of recognition, misophonia has been linked to altered brain activity in the auditory cortex and salience network (Schröder et al., 2019), and its neural basis includes the sensory motor system (Kumar et al., 2017; 2021). Research indicates that the degree of exposure does not alter the emotional response in misophonia, suggesting that exposure therapy is unlikely to be an effective treatment (Rosenthal et al., 2022). One study found that individuals with misophonia share traits with those on the autism spectrum (Rinaldi et al., 2023), supporting a sensory regulation-based approach to the condition. Furthermore, accommodations for misophonia have proven beneficial in educational settings and could offer similar advantages in workplaces (Porcaro et al., 2019). While some statistical evidence suggests the helpfulness of Cognitive Behavioral Therapy (CBT) for misophonia (Schröder, 2017; Jager et al., 2021), it is crucial to consider the community's perceptions and differentiate between various CBT approaches. Some CBT practitioners aim to help individuals modify their beliefs about triggers and adapt to living with them, while other practitioners might employ exposure therapy. There is no one-size-fits-all CBT solution. When treating and conceptualizing misophonia, it is essential to remember that "To date, no randomized controlled trials evaluating treatments for misophonia have been published" (Brout et al., 2018).

Sensory-regulation is defined as "the ability to select and process sensory information to plan and perform appropriate behaviors" (Piccardi and Gliga, 2022). In this context, behavior is driven by neurophysiological and sensory needs, rather than solely by cognitive needs (Dunn, 2014). Self-regulation refers to the capacity to manage one's own physiological states and choose behaviors in alignment with these states (Shanker and Barker, 2016). For the purpose of this discussion, "sensory regulation" specifically refers to the ability to calm the nervous system when triggered by sensory stimuli. When learning about misophonia, it is important to understand that our physical and emotional reactions to sensory stimuli are often caused by the stimuli themselves and the resulting fight-flight-freeze response, rather than being controlled by our initial thoughts and emotions. For an individual with misophonia, a sound is heard and the brain (specifically the amygdala) interprets this sound as a threat. This immediate perception of a threat then triggers an emotional and physiological response. This explains why consciously "thinking away" the trigger is ineffective; the cognitive thought process only engages after the misophonic reaction has already begun. The precise reason why these particular sounds provoke a fight-flight-freeze response remains unknown. Most people do not immediately associate emotional reactions with a specific narrative or story. For instance, the very first time someone is triggered by something is often not a memorable event. However, over time, negative associations with these triggers can develop, perhaps linked to interactions with family and friends or specific locations where triggers occurred. Nevertheless, the emotional response itself typically follows the initial fight-flight-freeze response.

When the brain and body enter a fight-flight-freeze state, there are only three possible reactions. In the context of misophonia, "fight" rarely escalates to physical violence, except possibly in very young children. Instead, it might manifest as feelings of anger and disgust, or a sharp verbal request for the person to stop. "Flight" is straightforward: many individuals with misophonia will leave the environment if they are able to escape the trigger. "Freeze" can be more perplexing for both the individual experiencing it and those around them. This can involve feeling paralyzed, unable to react, or even staring intensely at the source of the trigger. Consider if you were in a room with an unknown person wielding a knife in your direction—you would likely not take your eyes off the knife. The fight-flight-freeze response is our body's inherent mechanism for identifying and managing threats. For reasons not yet understood, misophonia causes this release of adrenaline, leading to distress upon hearing a trigger sound. Habituation, the process of becoming accustomed to a state or stimulus, does not occur in individuals with misophonia; their nervous systems simply do not adapt to the triggering sounds or visuals. The Autonomic Nervous System (ANS) is a vital and intricate part of the body that governs the fight-flight-freeze response, alongside other essential physiological functions. According to Waxenbaum (2023),

"The autonomic nervous system is a component of the peripheral nervous system that regulates involuntary physiologic processes including heart rate, blood pressure, respiration, digestion, and sexual arousal. It contains three anatomically distinct divisions: sympathetic, parasympathetic, and enteric." LeBouef (2023) further explains that "The autonomic nervous system (ANS) is made up of pathways of neurons that control various organ systems inside the body, using many diverse chemicals and signals to maintain homeostasis. It divides into the sympathetic and parasympathetic systems. The sympathetic component is better known as 'fight or flight' and the parasympathetic component as 'rest and digest.' It functions without conscious control throughout the lifespan of an organism to control cardiac muscle, smooth muscle, and exocrine and endocrine glands, which in turn regulate blood pressure, urination, bowel movements, and thermoregulation." The sympathetic division of the ANS is responsible for the fight-flight-freeze response. Conversely, the parasympathetic division is responsible for deactivating this response. The fight-flight-freeze response is initially detected by the amygdala, which then signals the hippocampus to activate the sympathetic nervous system. This activation leads to a rush of adrenaline, an elevated heart rate, and what is often described as an "anxious" feeling. The parasympathetic system then works to cease this response, helping the body return to a state often referred to as "calm." The enteric system, which deals with digestion, will not be discussed further here. While it is established that individuals with misophonia experience a fight-flight-freeze response, the underlying cause remains unknown. More extensive research and brain-based studies are needed to fully uncover the origins of misophonia and its onset. Although the nervous system is crucial for understanding misophonia, it can be beneficial to avoid getting overly engrossed in complex neurophysiological processes, especially given the preliminary nature of this research. However, for those interested in exploring the brain basis of misophonia further, a valuable starting point is the study by Dr. Sukhbinder Kumar:

Kumar, S., Tansley-Hancock, O., Sedley, W., Winston, J.S., Callaghan, M.F., Allen, M., Cope, T.E., Gander, P.E., Bamiou, D.E., & Griffiths, T.D. (2017). The brain basis for misophonia. Current Biology, 27(4).

Cognitive Behavioral Therapy (CBT) for Misophonia

Misophonia Psychoeducation

While this book is not primarily a psychoeducation tool concerning the background of misophonia, there are some things that are important to mention either as a review or as an introduction to the disorder. Misophonia is most-likely a neurophysiological condition where auditory (and sometimes visual stimuli) cause a fight-flight-freeze response to these stimuli (Brout, 2018). Misophonia was first coined in 2001 by audiologists Jastreboff and Jastreboff who noted that misophonic symptoms were different from hyperacusis and tinnitus (Jastreboff & Jastreboff, 2001). The following are a non-exhaustive list of common misophonia triggers which are useful to consider as a clinician or as a sufferer with misophonia. I have not listed visual triggers here as more research is necessary to identify the nature of visual triggers and misophonia (Schröder, 2013); however, I will list them in their own section. Misophonia triggers have been noted in existing literature. (Schröder, 2013; Rouw & Erfanian, 2018).

Common Misophonia Triggers

- Whistling
- Chewing
- Sniffling
- Snoring
- Lawn mowers/lawn equipment
- Sneezing

- Tapping
- Pen-clicking
- Deep heavy bass
- Styrofoam being rubbed
- The clicking of shoes
- Typing
- Mouse clicks when operating a computer
- The sound of air sucking in
- Gum-chewing
- Sucking sounds
- Licking

In this text, I may refer to the initial sensory input that precedes the autonomic and emotional cascade in misophonia as the *preceptory event*. This term differentiates the *raw perceptual trigger* (e.g., a sound like chewing or sniffing) from the subsequent physiological, emotional, and behavioral response. The goal of introducing this language is to name the precise moment of stimulus recognition— before conscious appraisal, but after sensory detection.

Many sounds that cause the preceptory event, otherwise known as the "trigger" for misophonia, are unavoidable. The nature of why these particular sounds cause a fight-flight-freeze reaction is yet to be fully understood from a neurological or physiological standpoint. What we do know is that the amygdala and fight-flight-freeze response are activated within milliseconds when this trigger sound is heard (Kumar, 2018; 2021).

Visual Triggers

Visual triggers associated with misophonia have been dubbed 'misokinesia'. This phenomenon can happen in instances where normally there would be an audial trigger (for example, watching a silent video of chewing), or isolated from any audial component (leg jiggling and shaking). More research is necessary to determine if *misokinesia* is part of the same disorder as misophonia, a co-occurring condition, or something else entirely. It is also currently unknown if there is a difference in sensory processing for visual triggers that are related to sounds and visual triggers that are unrelated to sounds.

Common visual triggers for misophonia include the following:

- Swaying
- Leg shaking
- Tapping
- Snapping
- Improper grammar like "u" "ur" "wut"
- Blinking text cursor (caret |)

While I do not know the exact nature of visual triggers as they relate to misophonia, I do know that many individuals with misophonia suffer from both—myself included. While the title of this book and its contents are mainly specifically tailored to *auditory* triggers, I will also focus on visual triggers so that those who struggle with visual triggers are not ignored. There is far less information on visual triggers, and thus I am including it regardless of a lack of research—although this research is growing (Schröder, 2013).

Understanding Sound and Frequency

When considering noise, our minds often turn to familiar examples like television static or the hum of a fan. However, noise possesses various "colors" with each characterized by distinct frequency profiles. These designations are not arbitrary; rather, they are grounded in acoustic science and find application in areas such as sleep enhancement, sound masking, tinnitus relief, and sensory regulation. Let us explore the most common noise colors and their unique properties.

White noise incorporates all frequencies perceptible to the human ear, with each frequency presented at equal intensity. Its auditory characteristic is a steady "hiss" and it is frequently employed to mask background sounds, thereby assisting with concentration or sleep. Common examples include the static from a television or radio and the hum of a fan or air conditioner. White noise is widely utilized for improving sleep quality, enhancing focus, and obscuring disruptive sounds in both work environments and during nighttime hours.

Pink noise is characterized by a deeper quality than white noise due to its emphasis on lower frequencies, resulting in a more balanced and calming auditory experience. Unlike white noise, pink noise often mirrors natural sounds and is generally perceived as less sharp. Examples include the steady sound of rainfall, the rhythmic rush of ocean waves, and the gentle rustling of leaves. Pink noise is frequently applied in sleep studies, meditation practices, and sound therapy, with its natural sound quality potentially contributing to improved sleep by influencing brain wave activity.

Brown noise, also known as red noise, exhibits an even greater concentration of energy in the lower frequencies compared to pink noise, producing a deep, rumbling sound. Its nomenclature derives from Brownian motion, a pattern of random movement, and bears no relation to the color brown. Auditory examples include distant thunder, the powerful roar of a strong waterfall, and the low rumbling of heavy engines. Brown noise may facilitate relaxation, reduce feelings of anxiety, and enhance sleep, particularly for individuals who prefer deeper, bass-rich sounds.

Green noise primarily encompasses mid-range frequencies and is said to closely resemble natural outdoor sounds. Some descriptions characterize it as the "gentle ambiance" of natural environments. This can manifest as the general sound of a forest, gentle ocean waves, or the soft whisper of a light breeze. Green noise is often employed in meditation, nature-based relaxation techniques, and sound therapy to cultivate a calming atmosphere.

Blue noise, or azure noise, accentuates higher frequencies, resulting in a sharper and more "hissy" auditory quality than white or pink noise, containing less energy in the lower frequency range. Examples include the sharp hiss of a spray can, the explosive sound of cymbal crashes, and high-pitched electronic signals. Blue noise is sometimes utilized in audio engineering, particularly in digital dithering, a process designed to smooth out sound distortions.

Violet noise, also known as purple noise, exhibits an even greater concentration of energy in the higher frequencies than blue noise. It presents a very sharp auditory quality and is occasionally used to mask high-pitched ringing in the ears, a condition known as tinnitus. Its characteristics include high-pitched whines and sharp hissing sounds. Violet noise finds application in tinnitus management and sound engineering to mask high-frequency disturbances.

Gray noise is engineered to sound equally loud across different frequencies, taking into account the sensitivity of human hearing. It achieves a balance that compensates for natural auditory perception. Examples of its use include audio simulations in hearing tests and noise employed in auditory training and sound therapy. Gray noise is utilized in psychoacoustic studies and therapeutic interventions involving auditory processing.

Black noise fundamentally represents the absence of sound or extremely low-energy noise. It may consist of periods of silence interspersed with very low-frequency sounds. This can be experienced as deep silence in very quiet environments, the subtle rumble of low-frequency seismic activity, or very distant, indistinct rumbling sounds. Black noise is associated with quiet spaces, profound silence, and in some contexts, infrasound research.

Orange noise is a rarer and more niche category that targets specific frequencies while simultaneously suppressing others. While less common, it is occasionally used in scientific experiments or specialized soundproofing applications. This might involve frequency-suppressed sounds in acoustics research or specialized noise employed in testing environments. Orange noise is sometimes applied in soundproofing, acoustics experiments, or auditory testing.

Each category of noise interacts with the auditory system in distinct ways, influencing our perception of sound and our experience of the surrounding environment. Some noise types, such as pink or brown noise, may contribute to improved sleep, while others, like blue or violet noise, may help reduce auditory disturbances. For individuals navigating sensory sensitivities, noise sensitivities, or conditions like misophonia, an understanding of different noise types can facilitate the identification of sounds that offer soothing and regulatory benefits to the nervous system.

Cognitive Behavioral Therapy (CBT) for Misophonia

Worksheet: Sound Masking

Instructions: In your internet browser, go to
https://www.misophoniasupport.com/sound-library/ and
listen to the four types of sound: pink, white, brown, and
green. Fill out the following chart as you listen to these
sounds. You can listen for as little as 1 minute or as long as
1 hour depending on your preference for the exercise.

Sound Name	How it made me feel	Would this sound help mask trigger noises?	Would I use this sound in my day-to-day life?
Pink			
White			
Brown			
Green			

Cognitive Behavioral Therapy (CBT) for Misophonia

Example: Sound Masking

Instructions: In your internet browser, go to https://www.misophoniasupport.com/sound-library/ and listen to the four types of sound: pink, white, brown, and green. Fill out the following chart as you listen to these sounds. You can listen for as little as 1 minute or as long as 1 hour depending on your preference for the exercise.

Sound Name	How it made me feel	Would this sound help mask trigger noises?	Would I use this sound in my day-to-day life?
Pink	Relaxed and calm.	Yes, I think so.	Yes, I would.
White	Nervous, felt too aggressive.	No.	No.
Brown	I felt neutral, not better or worse.	Not sure, maybe?	Probably not.
Green	It made me uncomfortable.	No.	No.

Cognitive Behavioral Therapy (CBT) for Misophonia

Adaption not Manipulation

For parents of misophonic children, romantic partners, friends, and educators, some traits of misophonia might look to them as manipulative behavior. For those with misophonia, when we are in fight-flight-freeze mode and dysregulated, our brains and bodies are telling us to do *anything* to stop the trigger—just as I imagine one would in any scenario that the brain and body have earmarked as a threat. It should be no surprise that when faced with an extremely aversive reaction to sounds (or visuals), a person with misophonia would go to extreme lengths to stop the noise. Examples of this might include creating alternative explanations to try and force the event not to happen. For example, one might say they cannot go out because they must do x, y, or z. Perhaps a partner goes to great lengths to avoid date night, even cancelling with excuses. Maybe the person invents a story for why something cannot be in their presence—for example, they might respond to gum chewers by saying that they are allergic to the smell. A parent with misophonia may tell their child that their loud chewing is rude, which is socially true in many circumstances, but this might not be the motivation for the request.

On the surface, these behaviors might seem manipulative. The definition of manipulate is to "control or influence a person or situation cleverly, unfairly, or unscrupulously." The key point here is "unfairness" or "unscrupulously". For persons with misophonia, it is not control of the other person that they want to achieve, but rather to alleviate or prevent a misophonic reaction. This behavior is adaptive. People with misophonia are accustomed to being ignored, ridiculed, and told that their condition is not real. Even those who feel supported might deal with guilt for asking others to stop a behavior due to misophonia and thus might rationalize an excuse that is to them more "logical," even if the receiving party suspects that misophonia is the cause.

An important part of misophonia is learning to self-advocate and adapt with the condition. However, for some, it can be harder, especially if the other party is not open to learning about their condition or accommodating it. Instead of thinking that people with misophonia are manipulative, let us consider that maybe they are just trying to avoid an unpleasant neurophysiological reaction, rather than controlling the person making the trigger for nefarious reasons.

Learning Your Tolerance Level

While there is no amount of *being triggered by misophonia* that is pleasant, most of us with the disorder have a level of stress and anxiety that we can handle before we go from fight-flight-freeze to a complete and utter sensory shutdown. Once we hit this level of tolerance, it can be difficult to bounce back, and some might even experience physical pain or flu-like symptoms. It is important to note that misophonia is worse when your overall stress and anxiety are bad. For example, when you are dealing with the loss of a loved one, school exams, or a work deadline, you are more likely to be triggered because you are not starting out at a baseline calm but rather are already in a heightened state of arousal before there is even a trigger!

For myself, I have identified which levels of stress I can tolerate and when I absolutely need to leave the environment. I use my smartwatch to track my overall heart rate and monitor my stress levels. While this is not an overly scientific measure, it is accurate enough to give insightful data on our fight-flight-freeze system. You can also use an Apple smartwatch, a Google smartwatch, a Fitbit device, or even a device from CVS or Amazon costing around $20 that will monitor your heart rate. Using a device to monitor your heart rate is useful as it does not rely on reported feelings which can be hard to parse in the moment. Some people freeze and feel numb, while others feel physical sensations. The use of a heart rate monitor removes this variability by simply relying on data over time. Most of these devices have apps that show historical data.

In my own case, my resting heart rate is roughly 76 to 80. As I become stressed and anxious, this rises to 90-100. While this level is uncomfortable, I am still able to function at a mostly tolerable level. Personally, I have identified a heart rate of 110-120 as my *breaking point* where I need to leave the room or situation immediately. Your own breaking point will be something you will have to determine by cross-referencing your distress to your heart rate and comparing data over time.

Worksheet: Monitoring Your Heart Rate

Instructions: Monitor your heart rate during times when you are in a neutral state and a triggered state and compare the results.

Monitor your heart rate once per day for one week while you are in a neutral calm state.

    1.
    2.
    3.
    4.
    5.
    6.

Monitor your heart rate once per day for one week while you are in an anxious state, but you are still able to stay in the room.

    1.
    2.
    3.
    4.
    5.
    6.

Monitor your heart rate while you are triggered and experiencing distress. Since this is hopefully less common and variable, simply do so when it happens and not at a set interval.

_____

_____

Compare the results to assess your baseline state, anxious state, and maximum tolerance level.

Baseline:

Anxious:

Maximum Tolerance:

Example: Monitoring Your Heart Rate

Instructions: Monitor your heart rate during times when you are in a neutral state and a triggered state and compare the results.

Monitor your heart rate once per day for one week while you are in a neutral calm state.

1. 78bpm
2. 75bpm
3. 80bpm
4. 85bpm
5. 87bpm
6. 87bpm

Monitor your heart rate once per day for one week while you are in an anxious state, but you are still able to stay in the room.

1. 97bpm
2. 95bpm
3. 91bpm
4. 96bpm
5. 95bpm
6. 97bpm

Monitor your heart rate while you are triggered and experiencing distress. Since this is hopefully less common and variable, simply do so when it happens and not at a set interval.

117bpm, 119bpm

Compare the results to assess your baseline state, anxious state, and maximum tolerance level.

Baseline: My baseline is between 75bpm to 87bpm

Anxious: My anxious baseline is between 91bpm to 97bpm

Maximum Tolerance: My maximum tolerance is between 117bpm and 119bpm

Misophonia Energy versus Happy Energy

Misophonia creates a situation where there is high energy (fight-flight-freeze) and the autonomic nervous system is going haywire with the worry that there is a threat. In a situation where a person is triggered by misophonia, there is high arousal and negative valence; whereas in a situation where a person is excited and happy such as during a dance party, their arousal is high, but their valence is positive (Brout, 2018). Dr. Jennifer Jo Brout expresses this phenomenon in her book *A Parent's Guide to Misophonia: Regulate, Reason, Reassure*. This explains how we can have *high arousal* in some situations and not be distressed.

There are situations where we can be upset (negative valence) and have low arousal—this is commonly called being "underresponsive" or "shutting down" in other conditions like sensory processing disorder/sensory integration or autism. It is useful to remember that our emotions and physiological reactions are more complex than just high arousal = fight-flight-freeze. The reality of disorders like misophonia is that emotions are a complex biological, physiological, hormonal, and cognitive mixture.

Cognitive Behavioral Therapy (CBT) for Misophonia

Worksheet: Your Tolerance Levels

Instructions: Reflect on and describe your different tolerance levels when experiencing misophonia.

Cognitive Behavioral Therapy (CBT) for Misophonia

Example: Your Tolerance Levels

I can't take any more and I am getting dizzy and feel sick.

My hands are shaking and I feel my heart beating heavily.

My chest feels heavy and my palms are sweating. This is just too much

Can't they stop making that sound, don't they know it hurts?

Should I leave the room or ask them to stop? It's all I can focus on.

I am uncomfortable— what is that sound? I want it to stop

Cognitive Behavioral Therapy (CBT) for Misophonia

Section 2: Misophonia Beliefs and Values

Core beliefs are beliefs that are deeply held by an individual. When misophonia intertwines with core beliefs, discrepancies can form that prevent coping skills or cause more distress for the individual. Core beliefs regarding misophonia can be related to 1) how well a person copes, 2) family and cultural considerations, 3) personal experiences regarding misophonia triggers. This is not an exhaustive list but does cover common areas that core beliefs about misophonia form. Core beliefs surrounding misophonia can be related to ways that parents, friends, and teachers have reacted to misophonia, or how a person adapts to misophonia as they live and grow.

Example core beliefs:

- I am crazy
- I will never enjoy life
- I cannot trust people
- I am better off alone
- I am broken

Since core beliefs are deeply held by individuals, they are not easily changed, and in many cases *the individual does not want to change this belief or worldview.* However, it can be useful to determine if the views that stem from this core belief are true. For example, consider the person with misophonia who believes they are a bad person because they do not enjoy spending time with their family when triggered. It can be useful to pick apart this thought. Is this person *actually* a bad person or are they experiencing a fight-flight-freeze reaction that is external to their worldview and belief system. While the answer may seem obvious to an outside party, focusing on the reality of the situation and evaluating beliefs as they relate to misophonia on a case-by-case basis is imperative for coping with misophonia.

Worksheet: Identify Your Core Beliefs

Instructions: Write three statements that you believe to be true about yourself or the world.

1. _____

2. _____

3. _____

Cognitive Behavioral Therapy (CBT) for Misophonia

Example: Identify Your Core Beliefs

Instructions: Write three statements that you believe to be true about yourself or the world.

1. *My worth depends on pleasing others.*

2. *I am a failure.*

3. *I am unlikeable and a bad friend.*

Cognitive Behavioral Therapy (CBT) for Misophonia

Intermediate Beliefs and Misophonia

Intermediate beliefs are beliefs that stem from core beliefs. An intermediate belief includes assumptions, values, personal rules, and ways of operating. For example, an intermediate belief about misophonia could be, "If I don't spend time with family, I am not a good person". The core belief of "my worth depends on pleasing others" has led to the intermediate belief that by letting down their family, they are not a good person. Intermediate beliefs are more likely to be changeable than core beliefs. The worksheets in this section are meant to help individuals with misophonia identify their beliefs as they relate to the condition. While these beliefs are not stemming from misophonia, they can impact how a person copes with misophonia. It can be useful to evaluate these beliefs and how they interact with misophonia.

Let us explore how intermediate beliefs—the rules we often live by—frequently stem from deeper, more fundamental core beliefs about ourselves and the world. Think of it like a tree: the leaves (intermediate beliefs) are visible and guide our daily actions, but they are firmly rooted in the trunk and roots (core beliefs). This connection is particularly relevant when working with individuals who experience misophonia, as their reactions to specific sounds can trigger a cascade from an intermediate belief to a core belief.

Take, for instance, the intermediate belief, "If I don't spend time with family, I am not a good person." This seemingly straightforward rule might be a direct reflection of a deeper core belief. Perhaps it is "I am not a good person unless I meet others' expectations," suggesting a struggle with external validation. Or it could stem from "My worth depends on how much I do for others," where self-worth is tied to constant self-sacrifice. For someone with misophonia, a family gathering with triggering sounds could activate this intermediate belief, leading to internal conflict: endure the sound and be a "good person," or avoid the sound and potentially feel like they are failing to meet expectations.

Consider another intermediate belief: "If I can't focus in class, I am not respecting my education, and I will fail." This belief, which can lead to intense anxiety, often has its origins in powerful core beliefs about one's capabilities. It could be rooted in the devastating thought, "I am a failure," where a single slip-up confirms a deeply held negative self-perception. Alternatively, it might come from "I'm not capable enough," a pervasive feeling of inadequacy that makes any academic challenge feel overwhelming and potentially catastrophic. For a student with misophonia, the inability to concentrate due to triggering sounds in a classroom could intensely activate this belief, spiraling into feelings of academic failure or inadequacy.

Finally, let us look at the intermediate belief, "If I am annoyed by my friend, I am not a good friend." This internal rule about friendship often points to profound core beliefs about self-worth and relationships. It might stem from the core belief, "I am a bad person," where any negative emotion or imperfection is seen as proof of an inherent flaw. Or it could be tied to "I am unworthy of close relationships if I have negative feelings," suggesting a fear that authentic emotions will lead to abandonment and isolation. For someone with misophonia, feeling intense annoyance towards a friend due to a triggering sound can be incredibly distressing, as it directly conflicts with this intermediate belief, potentially leading to guilt and a feeling of being a "bad friend" or unworthy of the relationship.

Understanding these connections between everyday rules and fundamental beliefs can be a powerful step in therapeutic work, particularly for those navigating the challenges of misophonia. By identifying and addressing these underlying core beliefs, individuals can begin to reframe their reactions and develop healthier coping mechanisms.

Worksheet: Identify Intermediate Beliefs

Instructions: Identify your intermediate beliefs, without considering how it impacts other areas of your life. Simply list three things that you believe to be true.

Intermediate Beliefs:

1. _____

2. _____

3. _____

Cognitive Behavioral Therapy (CBT) for Misophonia

Example: Identify Intermediate Beliefs

Instructions: Identify your intermediate beliefs, without considering how it impacts other areas of your life. Simply list three things that you believe to be true.

Intermediate Beliefs:

1. *If I don't spend time with family, I am not a good person.*
2. *If I can't focus in class, I am not respecting my education and I will fail.*
3. *If I am annoyed by my friend, I am not a good friend.*

Cognitive Behavioral Therapy (CBT) for Misophonia

Worksheet: Intermediate Beliefs and Misophonia

Instructions: For each intermediate belief, explain how it relates to your experience with misophonia.

Intermediate belief:

_____
_____
_____

How this belief relates to misophonia:

_____
_____
_____

Intermediate belief:

_____
_____
_____

How this belief relates to misophonia:

_____
_____
_____

Intermediate belief:

_____
_____
_____

How this belief relates to misophonia:

_____
_____
_____

Cognitive Behavioral Therapy (CBT) for Misophonia

Example: Intermediate Beliefs and Misophonia

Intermediate belief: *If I don't spend time with family, I am not a good person.*

How this belief relates to misophonia: *I don't spend time with family because I am triggered by their chewing, so I am a bad person.*

Intermediate belief: If I can't focus in class, I am not respecting my education and I will fail.

How this belief relates to misophonia: *My classmate clicks their pen and I can't focus on class. I am not doing my best and I will fail the class.*

Intermediate belief: *If I am annoyed by my friend, I am not a good friend.*

How this belief relates to misophonia: *My friend sniffles a lot and it triggers my misophonia. This makes me not want to hang out with them so I am not a good friend.*

Cognitive Behavioral Therapy (CBT) for Misophonia

Worksheet: Relating Intermediate Beliefs to Core Beliefs

Instructions: For each intermediate belief, identify the underlying core belief it connects to.

Intermediate Belief:

_____

_____

Core Belief:

_____

_____

Intermediate Belief:

_____

_____

Core Belief:

_____

_____

Intermediate Belief:

_____

_____

Core Belief:

_____

_____

Cognitive Behavioral Therapy (CBT) for Misophonia

Example: Relating Intermediate Beliefs to Core Beliefs

Intermediate Belief: *If I don't spend time with family, I am not a good person.*
Core Belief: *I am not a good person unless I meet others' expectations.*

Intermediate Belief: *If I can't focus in class, I am not respecting my education and I will fail.*
Core Belief: *I am a failure.*

Intermediate Belief: *If I am annoyed by my friend, I am not a good friend.*
Core Belief: *I am unworthy of close relationships if I have negative feelings.*

Cognitive Behavioral Therapy (CBT) for Misophonia

Values

Our values are things that we want in life. Values can come from core beliefs (culture, religion, family), but they can also come from physiological and psychological needs, adaptation to one's environment, and more. For example, some people may value time with family—whereas others who have less familial bonds might value peaceful time alone. There is no right or wrong value, and it can be helpful to consider one's values to pinpoint goals for coping with misophonia. It can be useful to first *consider values more generally* before considering how they relate to misophonia. Values will vary from person to person and should not be influenced by a parent or clinician. It is imperative that these values come from the person with misophonia. After values are determined, it can be helpful to consider how they relate *specifically* to misophonia. This insightful process helps the person with misophonia to determine how their values might relate to the symptoms of misophonia.

Cognitive Behavioral Therapy (CBT) for Misophonia

Worksheet: Determining Personal Values

Instructions: List three personal values that are important to you.

1. _____

2. _____

3. _____

Cognitive Behavioral Therapy (CBT) for Misophonia

Example: Determining Personal Values

Instructions: List three personal values that are important to you.

1. *Emotional control*
2. *Drama free relationships*
3. *Time alone to recharge*

Cognitive Behavioral Therapy (CBT) for Misophonia

Worksheet: How Values Relate to Misophonia

Instructions: For each value, describe how it connects to or is impacted by your misophonia.

1. **Value:** _____

   How it relates to misophonia:

   _____

2. **Value:** _____

   How it relates to misophonia:

   _____

3. **Value:** _____
   How it relates to misophonia:

   _____

Cognitive Behavioral Therapy (CBT) for Misophonia

Example: How Values Relate to Misophonia

1. **Value:** *Emotional control*

   How it relates to misophonia: *Being able to control emotions makes it easier to cope with the negative thoughts that occur after being triggered by misophonia*

2. **Value:** *Drama free relationships*

   How it relates to misophonia: *Misophonia causes conflict, so having relationships where there is less worry about safety is important*

3. **Value:** *Time alone to recharge*

   How it relates to misophonia: *Since misophonia leads to emotional exhaustion, the ability to have time alone to recharge is necessary to recover and calm down*

Cognitive Behavioral Therapy (CBT) for Misophonia

Section 3: The Impact of Misophonia

A common part of CBT is considering the *situation* which is causing the response that the individual experiencing symptoms seeks to alleviate. For misophonia, this can be difficult since there is no psychological control over the fight-flight-freeze mechanism. While a person with agoraphobia or another cognitive disorder might find relief from exposure therapy—for misophonia this will make things worse due to the physiological nature of the trigger moment. This is not to say that the person with misophonia has no control, but that control is limited by the nature of the condition.

Examples of situations where misophonia is the cause of distress for an individual.

1. When sitting in a classroom, another individual begins clicking their pen.
2. While standing in line at a supermarket, another individual begins whistling.
3. While eating dinner with family, chewing noises become unbearable.

The above is not an exhaustive list of situations that can trigger misophonia, but it does consider common triggers that are mentioned in research (Brout, 2018) and in personal stories. I am personally triggered by the first two of these and can attest that these situations are very uncomfortable for me.

Misophonia Triggers

The word "trigger" is commonly used to indicate a precipitating event that causes the misophonic fight-flight-freeze reaction. It is useful to understand the word *trigger* itself as this is not referring to a cognitive event causing a reaction. The word "trigger" has been commonly used in mental health pop culture and academic literature to examine a moment that causes an emotional reaction, but in the case of misophonia we are describing something entirely different. Triggers for misophonia concern specific sounds (or visuals) such as whistling, chewing, snapping, and sneezing wherein these otherwise normal stimuli produce a distressing response. Examining the exact triggers an individual has for misophonia is an important part of coping with the disorder.

Cognitive Behavioral Therapy (CBT) for Misophonia

Worksheet: My Misophonia Triggers

Instructions: List the sounds (and visuals if you wish) that trigger a fight-flight-freeze response for you. This does not have to be an exhaustive list but mention as many as you can remember.

-
-
-
-
-
-
-
-
-
-
-
-
-
-
-
-
-
-
-
-

Cognitive Behavioral Therapy (CBT) for Misophonia

Example: My Misophonia Triggers

Instructions: List the sounds (and visuals if you wish) that trigger a fight-flight-freeze response for you. This does not have to be an exhaustive list but mention as many as you can remember.

- *Whistling*
- *Chewing*
- *Coughing*
- *Pen clicking*
- *Snorting*
- *Nails clicking*

Cognitive Behavioral Therapy (CBT) for Misophonia

Worksheet: My Top 5 Misophonia Triggers

Instructions: Name the top 5 triggers for misophonia that cause you the most distress or arise most often for you day to day. You do not have to list them in any order.

1. _____

2. _____

3. _____

4. _____

5. _____

Cognitive Behavioral Therapy (CBT) for Misophonia

Example: My Top 5 Misophonia Triggers

Instructions: Name the top 5 triggers for misophonia that cause you the most distress or arise most often for you day to day. You do not have to list them in any order.

1. _Whistling_

2. _Tapping_

3. _Pen clicking_

4. _Nails clicking_

5. _Coughing_

Cognitive Behavioral Therapy (CBT) for Misophonia

Worksheet: Thinking About Triggers

Instructions: Reflect on your experiences with "new" triggers, including your feelings and potential impacts.

1. **When was the last time you remember having a "new" trigger?**

   _____

   _____

   _____

   _____

2. **How did it feel having a "new" trigger?**

   _____

   _____

   _____

   _____

3. **Are you afraid of having new triggers?**

   _____

   _____

   _____

   _____

4. **How would it impact you if you had more/new triggers?**

   _____

   _____

   _____

   _____

Cognitive Behavioral Therapy (CBT) for Misophonia

Example: Thinking About Triggers

Instructions: Reflect on your experiences with "new" triggers, including your feelings and potential impacts.

1. **When was the last time you remember having a "new" trigger?**

   The last time I remember having a new trigger was 5 years ago when I suddenly couldn't stand the sound of nail clipping.

2. **How did it feel having a "new" trigger?**

   I felt scared and frustrated that I had a new trigger... I didn't like suddenly reacting, and it made me very upset.

3. **Are you afraid of having new triggers?**

   Yes. It feels like I might eventually be triggered by every sound, and I don't know what I'd do.

4. **How would it impact you if you had more/new triggers?**

   I guess it would just make everyday life harder... I don't know how I'd escape if more sounds were triggers.

Cognitive Behavioral Therapy (CBT) for Misophonia

Section 4: Automatic Thoughts and Their Patterns

Automatic thoughts are the quick first thoughts that we have in a situation. For persons with misophonia, these automatic thoughts are impacted by the negative reaction to the uncontrollable fight-flight-freeze response. I want to emphasize that while automatic thoughts are a cognitive response, they are often a reaction to the physiological. For example, the fight-flight-freeze response is causing distress which the cognitive part of the brain is now interpreting through automatic thoughts.

This is an example of a bottom-up process: the body reacts first (with a fight-flight-freeze response) and the mind follows by making sense of that distress through automatic thoughts. In contrast, a top-down process starts with thoughts or beliefs influencing emotions and bodily responses. With misophonia, the intense physiological reaction often comes before any conscious thought, highlighting the need to address both the body and the mind in coping strategies.

Automatic thoughts and cognitive distortions are closely related concepts in cognitive behavioral therapy (CBT), but they represent different aspects of the thought process. Automatic thoughts are the rapid, spontaneous, and often unconscious thoughts that pop into your mind in response to a situation. They are the immediate, gut-level reactions we have. Cognitive distortions, on the other hand, are the flawed or irrational patterns that automatic thoughts often follow. They are the underlying biases or errors in thinking that make the automatic thoughts negative or unhelpful. In essence, a cognitive distortion is the "how" and "why" behind an unhelpful automatic thought.

For a person with misophonia, this distinction is important. An automatic thought might be that "My coworker is tapping their pen, and it is making me so angry." This is the immediate, non-deliberate thought. The cognitive distortion behind this thought could be catastrophizing, where the person believes the tapping will escalate and they will lose control, or personalizing where they believe the coworker is doing it to intentionally bother them. While the automatic thought is the specific content ("I am angry"), the cognitive distortion is the flawed pattern of thinking that gives rise to that anger. By identifying and challenging the cognitive distortion, a person can learn to reframe the automatic thought and change their emotional and behavioral response.

Worksheet: Automatic Thoughts from Misophonia

1. **Situation:**

   _____

   _____

   Automatic Thought:

   _____

   _____

2. **Situation:**

   _____

   _____

   Automatic Thought:

   _____

   _____

3. **Situation:**

   _____

   _____

   Automatic Thought:

   _____

   _____

Cognitive Behavioral Therapy (CBT) for Misophonia

Example: Automatic Thoughts from Misophonia

1. **Situation:** _When sitting in a classroom, another individual begins clicking their pen._

   Automatic thought: _Why are they clicking their pen, it's so annoying and rude._

2. **Situation:** _While standing in line at a supermarket, another individual begins whistling._

   Automatic Thought: _What is that? I hate it._

3. **Situation:** _While eating dinner with family, chewing noises become unbearable._

   Automatic Thought: _Why do you have to chew so loud? It's disgusting._

Cognitive Behavioral Therapy (CBT) for Misophonia

Worksheet: Misophonia Automatic Thoughts

Instructions: Write thoughts you automatically have when triggered by misophonia. (Either in the moment or from memory).

Cognitive Behavioral Therapy (CBT) for Misophonia

Example: Misophonia Automatic Thoughts

Why do sounds make me crazy?

Why are they so rude?

I just want it to stop.

I'm weird

Cognitive Behavioral Therapy (CBT) for Misophonia

Thought Patterns and Beliefs

Our thought patterns are ways that we think over time. For example, a person who is prone to catastrophizing will jump to conclusions such as "because I am triggered right now, the entire day is ruined," or a person experiencing all or nothing thinking may think that "because this feels bad right now, nothing will ever feel good again." Persons with misophonia may also attribute their triggers to malice regardless of actual known intent. For example, a person with misophonia may believe that "they are clicking their pen on purpose" when experiencing a triggering moment.

Our thought patterns are a useful way to categorize how our automatic thoughts normally occur. Automatic thoughts can follow a specific pattern such as catastrophizing, all or nothing thinking, mind-reading and assuming intent, and more. By recognizing our automatic thought patterns, we can then identify whether or not these types of thinking are adaptive or maladaptive ways to respond to the precipitating event (the misophonic trigger moment). The following worksheets are meant to help persons with misophonia identify their patterns and beliefs related to the condition.

The cognitive distortions described in the included image are a key component of Aaron Beck's work in cognitive behavioral therapy (CBT). They are essentially biased or irrational ways of thinking that can lead to negative emotions, unhelpful behaviors, and a distorted view of reality. Understanding these thought patterns is the first step in learning to challenge and change them.

All-or-nothing thinking

This distortion involves thinking in absolute, black-and-white terms without any room for shades of gray. You see yourself as either a complete success or a total failure, with no middle ground. For someone with misophonia, this might manifest as "I cannot go to that movie theater; if I hear even one popcorn crunch, my entire evening will be ruined, and so there is no point in going." This thought pattern prevents you from seeing a situation as having both positive and negative aspects.

Catastrophizing

Catastrophizing is the act of predicting a dire, worst-case scenario for a future event. It involves exaggerating the consequences of a situation and assuming that a difficult event will be completely unbearable. For a person with misophonia, this could be thinking "This person is chewing their gum so loudly that I just know it is going to drive me so crazy that I will have a panic attack right here in the office and I will wind up getting fired." The severity of the anticipated outcome is far beyond the reality of the situation.

Shoulds and musts

This distortion involves holding rigid, unbending rules about how you or others should behave. When these rules are broken, you feel angry, frustrated, or disappointed. A misophonia sufferer might think that "People **should** know not to slurp their drinks in a quiet library. It is so rude, and they **must** be doing it just to be annoying." This kind of thinking leads to feelings of resentment and makes it difficult to accept imperfections in others.

Overgeneralizing

This is a thought pattern where you take a single negative event and assume it will happen again and again, across all situations. It is like using one bad experience to paint a broad, negative picture of everything. Someone with misophonia who overgeneralizes might have one difficult airplane flight where someone loudly crunched on ice and then conclude that "I can never fly again. Every flight will be filled with irritating noises that make me miserable."

Personalizing

Personalizing is the tendency to believe that you are the cause of an external event, especially a negative one, even when you are not responsible. It is a form of taking things personally. For misophonia, this can lead to the belief that the person making the sound is doing it to intentionally bother you, rather than just being unaware. For example, "My neighbor is drilling at this late hour just to get on my nerves."

Mental filtering

This distortion involves picking out one negative detail in a situation and dwelling on it exclusively, to the point that your vision of reality becomes clouded by that one negative. It is like having a mental filter that blocks out all positive information. A person with misophonia might be at a wonderful party, but if they hear a single person chewing loudly, their mind will fixate on that one sound, making them unable to enjoy the conversations, food, or company.

Dismissing the positive

Dismissing the positive is a way of neutralizing or invalidating positive experiences. You might receive a compliment, but you immediately brush it off. When applied to misophonia, this might look like someone at a beautiful beach who is so bothered by the crunching of the sand under someone's feet that they ignore the calming sound of the waves and the beautiful sunset.

Cognitive labeling

This distortion involves applying a broad, negative label to yourself or others based on a single action. It is an extreme form of overgeneralizing. Instead of thinking "That person is slurping their coffee," you label them as "a disgusting, inconsiderate person." This makes it hard to see people as complex individuals and instead reduces them to a single perceived flaw.

Jumping to conclusions

This is a common cognitive distortion that involves making an assumption without having all the facts. It often includes two sub-distortions: mindreading and fortune-telling. When you jump to conclusions with misophonia, you might hear a sound and immediately create a story about the situation and the person involved, even though you have no evidence.

Mindreading

This is a form of jumping to conclusions where you assume you know what another person is thinking or feeling. With misophonia, you might hear someone sniffling and automatically think that "They are doing this on purpose to annoy me," without considering other possibilities such as allergies or a cold.

Fortune-telling

This is the second form of jumping to conclusions, where you predict that an event will turn out badly without any evidence. For someone with misophonia, this could be thinking that "I am going to a dinner party tonight. I know someone will be a loud chewer, and it is going to ruin my entire night." This thought can cause anxiety and stress before the event even starts.

Identify with emotions

This distortion is the belief that your feelings are an absolute truth about who you are. Instead of recognizing that emotions are temporary states, you believe that how you feel at a given moment defines you. For a person with misophonia, this could mean thinking that "I feel so angry and out of control when I hear that sound, so I must be an angry, out-of-control person." This makes it difficult to see that you can manage your reactions and that the emotion does not define your entire personality.

Worksheet: All-or-Nothing Thinking

Instructions: Read the statements below and identify the black-and-white thinking. Then, reframe each thought to include a more balanced perspective.

All-or-nothing thought: *"I can't go to the movie theater because if I hear even one person crunching on popcorn, my whole night will be ruined."*

Reframed thought:

_____

_____

All-or-nothing thought: *"I made a mistake at work, so I'm a total failure and will probably be fired."*

Reframed thought:

_____

_____

Cognitive Behavioral Therapy (CBT) for Misophonia

Example: All-or-Nothing Thinking

Instructions: Read the statements below and identify the black-and-white thinking. Then, reframe each thought to include a more balanced perspective.

All-or-nothing thought: *"I can't go to the movie theater because if I hear even one person crunching on popcorn, my whole night will be ruined."*

Reframed thought: *Going to the movie might be challenging, but I can cope with the noise. Even if I get frustrated by a sound, it won't ruin my entire night, and I can still find a way to enjoy the movie and the time out with friends.*

All-or-nothing thought: *"I made a mistake at work, so I'm a total failure and will probably be fired."*

Reframed thought: *I made a mistake, but everyone makes mistakes. It's a chance for me to learn and improve. One mistake doesn't define my entire career or make me a failure. I will correct the error and move on.*

Cognitive Behavioral Therapy (CBT) for Misophonia

Worksheet: Catastrophizing

Instructions: For each scenario, write the catastrophic thought that might arise from misophonia. Then, write a more realistic and grounded outcome.

Scenario: You hear someone loudly slurping their soup at a restaurant.

Catastrophic thought:

_____

_____

Realistic outcome:

_____

_____

Scenario: A co-worker is chewing gum loudly at their desk.

Catastrophic thought:

_____

_____

Realistic outcome:

_____

_____

Cognitive Behavioral Therapy (CBT) for Misophonia

Example: Catastrophizing

Instructions: For each scenario, write the catastrophic thought that might arise from misophonia. Then, write a more realistic and grounded outcome.

Scenario: You hear someone loudly slurping their soup at a restaurant.

Catastrophic thought: *The slurping is going to ruin my meal. I won't be able to enjoy it.*

Realistic outcome: *I may be able to apply coping mechanisms, and it won't be that bad.*

Scenario: A co-worker is chewing gum loudly at their desk.

Catastrophic thought: *There is no way I can get any work done with them chewing gum that loudly. My productivity will suffer.*

Realistic outcome: *They may not know they are chewing with their mouth open. I can mention it to them calmly and ask them to stop.*

Cognitive Behavioral Therapy (CBT) for Misophonia

Worksheet: Shoulds and Musts

Instructions: Identify the rigid "should" or "must" statement in each situation. Then, rewrite the statement to be more flexible and accepting.

Situation: You hear someone breathing heavily in a quiet room, and it makes you angry.

"Should" statement:

_____

_____

Flexible statement:

_____

_____

Situation: You feel frustrated when your family doesn't eat their dinner without making a sound.

"Should" statement:

_____

_____

Flexible statement:

_____

_____

Cognitive Behavioral Therapy (CBT) for Misophonia

Example: Shoulds and Musts

Instructions: Identify the rigid "should" or "must" statement in each situation. Then, rewrite the statement to be more flexible and accepting.

Situation: You hear someone breathing heavily in a quiet room, and it makes you angry.

"Should" statement: *People should know that they are breathing loudly.*

Flexible statement: *The person may not be aware of how loudly they are breathing.*

Situation: You feel frustrated when your family doesn't eat their dinner without making a sound.

"Should" statement: *Why can't these people eat silently?*

Flexible statement: *Sometimes you can't help but make noise while eating.*

Cognitive Behavioral Therapy (CBT) for Misophonia

Worksheet: Overgeneralizing

Instructions: Identify the overgeneralization in each thought. Then, provide a counterstatement that is specific and accurate.

Thought: "My last date was a nightmare because they were a loud eater. I'll never be able to date anyone again."

Overgeneralization:

_____

_____

Counterstatement:

_____

_____

Thought: "I had to leave a coffee shop because someone was tapping their pen. All public places are unbearable."

Overgeneralization:

_____

_____

Counterstatement:

_____

_____

Cognitive Behavioral Therapy (CBT) for Misophonia

Exercise: Overgeneralizing

Instructions: Identify the overgeneralization in each thought. Then, provide a counterstatement that is specific and accurate.

Thought: "*My last date was a nightmare because they were a loud eater. I'll never be able to date anyone again.*"

Overgeneralization: *One experience represents all future experiences.*

Counter-statement: *My next date may be sensitive to misophonia, and the next date might go well.*

Thought: "*I had to leave a coffee shop because someone was tapping their pen. All public places are unbearable.*"

Overgeneralization: *One experience representing all experiences in the future.*

Counter-statement: *The next coffee shop may not have anyone with pens.*

Cognitive Behavioral Therapy (CBT) for Misophonia

Worksheet: Personalizing

Instructions: In each scenario, identify the belief that the sound is being made to intentionally bother you. Then, offer an alternative, less personal explanation.

Scenario: Your roommate is rustling a bag of chips while you are trying to read.

Personalized thought:

_____

_____

Alternative explanation:

_____

_____

Scenario: You hear a neighbor stomping around upstairs.

Personalized thought:

_____

_____

Alternative explanation:

_____

_____

Cognitive Behavioral Therapy (CBT) for Misophonia

Example: Personalizing

Instructions: In each scenario, identify the belief that the sound is being made to intentionally bother you. Then, offer an alternative, less personal explanation.

Scenario: Your roommate is rustling a bag of chips while you are trying to read.

Personalized thought: *They know that rustling chips annoys me. Why are they doing this?*

Alternative explanation: *They forgot that I'm sensitive to the bag rustling.*

Scenario: You hear a neighbor stomping around upstairs.

Personalized thought: *The neighbor knows the stomping is a trigger for me. Why are they doing it?*

Alternative explanation: *The neighbor may not know they are stomping their feet.*

Cognitive Behavioral Therapy (CBT) for Misophonia

Worksheet: Mental Filtering

Instructions: For each scenario, describe what a misophonia sufferer might focus on (the negative) and what they are likely ignoring (the positive).

Scenario: You're at a family dinner filled with laughter and good conversation, but one person is chewing loudly.

Focusing on:

_____
_____

Ignoring:

_____
_____
_____

Scenario: You're on vacation at a beautiful resort, but you can hear a dripping faucet in your room.

Focusing on:

_____
_____

Ignoring:

_____
_____

Cognitive Behavioral Therapy (CBT) for Misophonia

Example: Mental Filtering

Instructions: For each scenario, describe what a misophonia sufferer might focus on (the negative) and what they are likely ignoring (the positive).

Scenario: You're at a family dinner filled with laughter and good conversation, but one person is chewing loudly.

Focusing on: _The loud chewing._

Ignoring: _The experience with family and good conversation._

Scenario: You're on vacation at a beautiful resort, but you can hear a dripping faucet in your room.

Focusing on: _The constant dripping of the faucet._

Ignoring: _The experience at a beautiful resort._

Cognitive Behavioral Therapy (CBT) for Misophonia

Worksheet: Dismissing the Positive

Instructions: Describe how a positive event could be turned into a negative one due to misophonia.

Positive Event: Your friend cooked a delicious meal just for you.

Dismissal:

_____
_____

Explanation:

_____
_____

Positive Event: You are relaxing and watching a movie with a loved one.

Dismissal:

_____
_____

Explanation:

_____
_____

Cognitive Behavioral Therapy (CBT) for Misophonia

Example: Dismissing the Positive

Instructions: Describe how a positive event could be turned into a negative one due to misophonia.

Positive Event: *Your friend cooked a delicious meal just for you.*
Dismissal: *My friend made a great meal, but they chewed too loudly while we were eating.*
Explanation: *The positive gesture of a friend cooking is completely overshadowed by the misophonia trigger of loud chewing. The individual's focus shifts from appreciating the meal and the kindness of the friend to an intense emotional reaction, such as anxiety or anger, caused by the sound.*

Positive Event: *You are relaxing and watching a movie with a loved one.*
Dismissal: *I couldn't relax during the movie because my loved one was eating popcorn and the sound was driving me crazy.*
Explanation: *The trigger sound of popcorn chewing prevents the individual from enjoying the relaxing, shared experience with their loved one. Instead of feeling calm and connected, they feel frustration and distress. The positive experience of the movie is dismissed, and the overwhelming feeling of the misophonia trigger takes over.*

169

Cognitive Behavioral Therapy (CBT) for Misophonia

Worksheet: Cognitive labeling

Instructions: Identify the negative label being applied to a person. Then, rephrase the thought to focus on the specific behavior instead of a blanket judgment of the person.

Labeling: "My co-worker is a disgusting person because they sniffle constantly."

The label:

_____
_____

Rephrased thought:

_____
_____

Labeling: "That person on the bus is a complete slob for biting their nails."

The label:

_____
_____

Rephrased thought:

_____
_____

Cognitive Behavioral Therapy (CBT) for Misophonia

Example: Cognitive labeling

Instructions: Identify the negative label being applied to a person. Then, rephrase the thought to focus on the specific behavior instead of a blanket judgment of the person.

Labeling: "My co-worker is a disgusting person because they sniffle constantly."

The label: *The coworker is judged on one action — sniffling.*

Rephrased thought: *Other than the sniffling, they are a great coworker, and I enjoy working with them.*

Labeling: "That person on the bus is a complete slob for biting their nails."

The label: *Biting of nails is disgusting.*

Rephrased thought: *They may be biting their nails as a coping mechanism.*

Cognitive Behavioral Therapy (CBT) for Misophonia

Worksheet: Jumping to conclusions

Instructions: Identify the conclusion that is made without full information. Then, list a few alternative possibilities that could also be true.

Conclusion: Your partner is chewing their food loudly. You immediately think they are doing it to provoke you because you have talked to them about it before.

The conclusion:

_____

_____

Alternative possibilities:

_____

_____

Cognitive Behavioral Therapy (CBT) for Misophonia

Exercise: Jumping to conclusions

Instructions: Identify the conclusion that is made without full information. Then, list a few alternative possibilities that could also be true.

Conclusion: Your partner is chewing their food loudly. You immediately think they are doing it to provoke you because you have talked to them about it before.

The conclusion: _They are purposely chewing loudly._

Alternative possibilities: _They may have a dental issue that prevents them from chewing quietly or they may be unaware of how they are chewing noisily._

Cognitive Behavioral Therapy (CBT) for Misophonia

Worksheet: Mindreading

Instructions: Identify the assumption being made about someone's thoughts or feelings. Then, write a neutral, fact-based statement.

Assumption: You are at a meeting, and someone starts clearing their throat. You think, "They're doing that because they think I talk too much."

Mindreading thought:

_____

_____

Fact-based statement:

_____

_____

Assumption: Your spouse sighs and you immediately think, "They're annoyed with me."

Mindreading thought:

_____

_____

Fact-based statement:

_____

_____

Cognitive Behavioral Therapy (CBT) for Misophonia

Example: Mindreading

Instructions: Identify the assumption being made about someone's thoughts or feelings. Then, write a neutral, fact-based statement.

Assumption: You are at a meeting, and someone starts clearing their throat. You think, "They're doing that because they think I talk too much."

Mindreading thought: *They are purposely clearing their throat to annoy me.*

Fact-based statement: *They may have a cold or may be taking medication that causes the throat clearing.*

Assumption: Your spouse sighs and you immediately think, "They're annoyed with me."

Mindreading thought: *They are annoyed with me.*

Fact-based statement: *They may be frustrated with something entirely unrelated.*

Cognitive Behavioral Therapy (CBT) for Misophonia

Worksheet: Fortune-Telling

Instructions: Write a predictive thought about a future event. Then, list a few ways the event could actually turn out that are not negative.

Prediction: "I have to attend a work lunch tomorrow. I just know someone will be a loud chewer, and I won't be able to handle it."

Prediction:

_____

_____

Alternative outcomes:

_____

_____

Prediction: "I have to visit my parents. I know my dad will slurp his coffee, and I'll get so angry it will ruin the whole visit."

Prediction:

_____

_____

Alternative outcomes:

_____

_____

Cognitive Behavioral Therapy (CBT) for Misophonia

Example: Fortune-Telling

Instructions: Write a predictive thought about a future event. Then, list a few ways the event could actually turn out that are not negative.

Prediction: "I have to attend a work lunch tomorrow. I just know someone will be a loud chewer, and I won't be able to handle it."

Prediction: _Someone will trigger my misophonia._

Alternative outcomes: _We will have a great lunch with good food and conversation._

Prediction: "I have to visit my parents. I know my dad will slurp his coffee, and I'll get so angry it will ruin the whole visit."

Prediction: _Dad will slurp his coffee._

Alternative outcomes: _Dad may not drink coffee around me and I will have a good visit._

Cognitive Behavioral Therapy (CBT) for Misophonia

Worksheet: Identify With Emotions

Instructions: Identify the thought that equates a temporary emotion with a permanent identity. Then, rephrase the statement to separate the feeling from your core identity.

Emotion-as-identity: "I am so angry when I hear that sound; I'm just an angry person."

The thought:

_____

_____

Rephrased thought:

_____

_____

Emotion-as-identity: "I feel so disgusted by that noise; I'm a disgusting person."

The thought:

_____

_____

Rephrased thought:

_____

_____

Cognitive Behavioral Therapy (CBT) for Misophonia

Example: Identify With Emotions

Instructions: Identify the thought that equates a temporary emotion with a permanent identity. Then, rephrase the statement to separate the feeling from your core identity.

Emotion-as-identity: "I am so angry when I hear that sound; I'm just an angry person."

The thought: _I am naturally angry all the time._

Rephrased thought: _My reaction doesn't define me. I get triggered by certain things._

Emotion-as-identity: "I feel so disgusted by that noise; I'm a disgusting person."

The thought_: I am disgusting since I react to noise._

Rephrased thought_: I react to the noise, but it doesn't make me disgusting overall._

Cognitive Behavioral Therapy (CBT) for Misophonia

Reactions to Triggers

How individuals react to misophonia triggers can vary from person to person. While the fight-flight-freeze mechanism is likely the same in each person with the disorder, we all have our own individual thoughts and experiences that change our misophonic experience. For example, if I am triggered by dogs barking—and have been attacked by a dog in the past—my reaction likely has another layer of fear and trauma involved. My automatic thought when hearing a dog bark (after the trigger moment) may be "that dog might attack me" even if there are no signs of attack. While this response is not *entirely* misophonia, that is the point.

We are all unique in our experiences and ways of looking at the world. For a person who believes that chewing with your mouth closed is proper etiquette, the misophonic response might be increased by the 'rudeness' of open mouth chewing, which can then lead to automatic thoughts such as "they should chew with their mouth closed". These reactions are something we can examine and process, whereas while we cannot change the moment of a misophonia trigger itself, we can work on our automatic thoughts and emotional responses.

Cognitive Behavioral Therapy (CBT) for Misophonia

Worksheet: My Reaction to Triggers

Instructions: Describe when your reactions to triggers feel worse or easier and explain the differences.

1. **Are there times where your reaction to triggers feels worse?**

   _____

   _____

   _____

   _____

   _____

2. **Are there times when your reaction to triggers feels easier?**

   _____

   _____

   _____

   _____

   _____

3. **What is the difference between times it feels worse and times it feels easier?**

   _____

   _____

   _____

   _____

   _____

Cognitive Behavioral Therapy (CBT) for Misophonia

Example: My Reaction to Triggers

Instructions: Describe when your reactions to triggers feel worse or easier and explain the differences.

1. **Are there times where your reaction to triggers feels worse?**

   I feel worse when I am tired or hungry, or if I had a bad day. For example, if I don't sleep well I am more sensitive and the triggers feel worse.

2. **Are there times when your reaction to triggers feels easier?**

   Sometimes the triggers are less intense if I am in a good mood, as for example I was at the beach last week having a good time and heard somebody chewing chips. I didn't like it, but I just went in the water and didn't think about it after.

3. **What is the difference between times it feels worse and times it feels easier?**

   When I'm tired or hungry my physiological needs aren't met and I'm also more stressed. At the beach I was in a good mood and the swimming might have also been a calming activity.

Cognitive Behavioral Therapy (CBT) for Misophonia

Worksheet: How I Feel About My Trigger

Instructions: For a chosen trigger, describe the sound/visual, its cause, whether it would bother you without misophonia, and if accommodation or removal is possible.

1. **What is the trigger sound/visual?**

    _____

    _____

    _____

    _____

2. **Why is this sound/visual happening?**

    _____

    _____

    _____

    _____

3. **If I didn't have misophonia would this sound/visual still bother me?**

    _____

    _____

    _____

    _____

4. **Is there a way I can remove myself from the sound/visual or ask for an accommodation?**

    _____

    _____

    _____

    _____

Cognitive Behavioral Therapy (CBT) for Misophonia

Example: How I Feel About My Trigger

Instructions: For a chosen trigger, describe the sound/visual, its cause, whether it would bother you without misophonia, and if accommodation or removal is possible.

1. **What is the trigger sound/visual?**

   The sound I am triggered by is commercial lawnmowers and yard work.

2. **Why is this sound/visual happening?**

   The lawnmowers are mowing the lawn so that it is kept maintained and there isn't overgrowth and wildlife.

3. **If I didn't have misophonia would this sound/visual still bother me?**

   I might be annoyed, but I don't think it would be painful or overly distressing.

4. **Is there a way I can remove myself from the sound/visual or ask for an accommodation?**

   I could leave the house while there's mowing and maybe go for a drive or go hang out with friends. I can't ask for accommodation because they have to mow our apartment yard. I could try noise cancelling headphones or earbuds if I can't leave.

Cognitive Behavioral Therapy (CBT) for Misophonia

Worksheet: Recognizing Thoughts While Triggered

Instructions: In the moment of the trigger, write your thoughts (immediate thoughts) in a note app or on paper.

1. _____

2. _____

3. _____

Cognitive Behavioral Therapy (CBT) for Misophonia

Example: Recognizing Thoughts While Triggered

Instructions: In the moment of the trigger, write your thoughts (immediate thoughts) in a note app or on paper.

1. *Why are they whistling? It's so rude.*

2. *Why do you chew like that? It's disgusting.*

3. *Why is this happening to me? It's so unfair.*

Cognitive Behavioral Therapy (CBT) for Misophonia

Worksheet: Matching Thoughts and Triggers

Instructions: Consider how you feel when faced with a specific trigger—what is your predominant thought? Match your triggers and thoughts either as you are triggered (keep a list) or as memories you have of thoughts. It can be helpful to do this in the moment, if possible, to get the most accurate *immediate* thought.

Trigger	Thought
Whistling	
Chewing	
Pen Clicking	

Cognitive Behavioral Therapy (CBT) for Misophonia

Example: Matching Thoughts and Triggers

Instructions: Consider how you feel when faced with a specific trigger—what is your predominant thought? Match your triggers and thoughts either as you are triggered (keep a list) or as memories you have of thoughts. It can be helpful to do this in the moment, if possible, to get the most accurate *immediate* thought.

Trigger	Thought
Whistling	*That's so rude, why are they doing that? I hate it.*
Chewing	*That sounds awful, why do they chew like a cow?*
Pen Clicking	*I think they're doing that on purpose to bother me.*

Cognitive Behavioral Therapy (CBT) for Misophonia

Reframing Misophonia

Reframing is a cognitive tool that is used to help cope with negative emotions. Although the trigger for misophonia happens before we have an emotional response, we can still reframe our beliefs about misophonia. The idea here is to write down our negative thoughts about misophonia and then re-write them in a way that no longer associates the origin of the trigger as the instigator.

Cognitive Behavioral Therapy (CBT) for Misophonia

Worksheet: Re-framing Misophonia

Instructions: Take a misophonia-related thought and re-frame it into a more helpful or adaptive thought.

Misophonia thought:

_____

_____

Misophonia thought re-framed:

_____

_____

Cognitive Behavioral Therapy (CBT) for Misophonia

Example: Re-framing Misophonia

Instructions: Take a misophonia-related thought and re-frame it into a more helpful or adaptive thought.

Misophonia thought: *Why did he have to whistle? It is so rude. I hate whistling. This is so cruel.*

Misophonia thought re-framed: *He probably does not know whistling upsets me. Maybe he is happy or trying to keep himself calm.*

Cognitive Behavioral Therapy (CBT) for Misophonia

Maladaptive versus Adaptive Coping Mechanisms

People with misophonia and sensory integration issues in general (think autism, sensory processing, etc.) create ways to cope without even thinking about it. Some of these coping methods are adaptive and some of them are maladaptive.

A maladaptive coping mechanism is when we find ways to cope that are counterproductive to the thing we are trying to cope with or otherwise harmful for health. Common maladaptive behaviors are unhealthy foods, cigarettes, drug misuse, alcohol abuse, gambling, and self-harm. This is not an exhaustive list but rather highlights that maladaptive coping mechanisms are not only unhelpful long-term, but often harmful.

On the other hand, an adaptive coping mechanism is something that is both helpful for misophonia and anxiety and also beneficial for the long-term health of the individual. Common examples of adaptive coping mechanisms include engaging in exercise, having a well-balanced nutritious diet, drinking water, and spending time in nature.

Cognitive Behavioral Therapy (CBT) for Misophonia

Is Avoidance Adaptive or Maladaptive?

Whether or not *avoidance* is a maladaptive coping mechanism is something that mental health professionals and researchers debate. In the view of some authors, avoidance is a maladaptive behavior because it can hinder social events and learning engagement and thus should be remedied. This view is simplistic and does not account for the lack of habituation that is shown in persons with misophonia. When we think of misophonia through the lens of sensory regulation and the fight-flight-freeze response, it is only natural that a person with misophonia would want to *avoid* a trigger or leave the room when it happens. The easiest way to not be distressed is to not be in the presence of the stressor!

Whether or not *avoidance* is maladaptive or adaptive depends on numerous factors, and almost all of them are up to the individual and by extension their families. Social expectations are largely cultural and whether something like family dinner is something to be adapted to and coped with or something that can be avoided will be situational. For some, the distress at mealtimes is so great that even the cultural will to eat dinner with one's family is not enough to overcome the urge to flee. It is important to not judge too harshly in these situations—even if it is yourself that you are judging.

There is a degree in which avoidance is a maladaptive coping mechanism, and that degree is whatever line the person with misophonia has drawn in the sand. For some, there are hard boundaries that cannot be crossed such as restaurants or movie theatres. For others, these lines are more nuanced and some days they can handle it and other days they cannot. This variance is to be expected when we consider self-regulation and remember that misophonia varies based on the physiological, cognitive, and emotional needs of a person, and not just on hard assumptions.

Of course, if a person with misophonia has become overly withdrawn, lonely, or is avoiding relationships with their friends and family altogether, this is a maladaptive behavior. However, it is possible that it is not necessarily misophonia causing this behavior, but rather a lack of accommodations and safety in the relationship which helps the person with misophonia stay present. Unfortunately, some triggers cannot be covered (such as the sound of a person's voice), so this can become tricky in these scenarios.

The answer to the question this chapter seeks to answer—"Is avoidance adaptive or maladaptive?"—is that it entirely depends on how often the person is avoiding, why they are avoiding, and whether or not it is leading to more distress for the individual who is doing the avoiding. While that answer might seem convoluted, it is also one that might change through negotiating accommodations and developing coping mechanisms.

Cognitive Behavioral Therapy (CBT) for Misophonia

Worksheet: Adaptive versus Maladaptive Coping Skills

Instructions: Describe past coping mechanisms, whether they helped, and alternative ways you could cope.

Adaptive Coping Skills	Maladaptive Coping Skills

Cognitive Behavioral Therapy (CBT) for Misophonia

Example: Adaptive versus Maladaptive Coping Skills

Instructions: Describe past coping mechanisms, whether they helped, and alternative ways you could cope.

Adaptive Coping Skills	Maladaptive Coping Skills
• Telling others about my misophonia and calmly asking for accommodations • Bringing my earphones or earbuds with me and using them when necessary • Using my coping skills worksheets to remember that I will be okay	• Hiding in my room all the time • Crying in public whenever there are sounds I don't like • Yelling at my family to stop making noises • Avoiding things that matter to me so I won't be triggered • Not telling people I have misophonia and instead shutting down or withdrawing completely

Cognitive Behavioral Therapy (CBT) for Misophonia

Personal and External Misophonia Beliefs

Both personal beliefs and external beliefs of those around us—and the wider world—are an important part of evaluating what misophonia means to an individual. These beliefs can impact how a person with misophonia lives their life, or how others around them react. This can lead to a lack of accommodation, to loneliness, or ideally to support and understanding.

Since persons with misophonia do not live in a bubble, the world at large and those we interact with daily can all influence our personal beliefs and behaviors regarding misophonia. For example, some families value family dinners more than others and it might be inexcusable to leave the dinner table regardless of triggers. This can often happen in families where parents *believe* that misophonia is *behavioral* rather than physiological. Sometimes well-meaning uneducated clinicians can perpetuate this view and will even suggest that *any form of avoidance* will make misophonia worse—something we have already rejected entirely. This is not to say that a person with misophonia triggered by chewing can never eat dinner with their family, but it might mean that there is a staggered schedule involving one night on and one night off, using earphones, or having white noise playing in the room.

Coping skills and adaptation are entirely dependent on the values and beliefs of the person with misophonia and those around them. I will caution that these beliefs can be changed and in the case of untrue beliefs—like the fact that misophonia will get worse if accommodated—should be remedied with psychoeducation, review of literature, and discussion with sufferers.

Worksheet: Beliefs About Misophonia

Instructions: Complete the sentences to express your feelings and beliefs about misophonia, including what you would call it.

Misophonia makes me feel:

_____
_____
_____
_____

If I didn't have misophonia I would:

_____
_____
_____
_____

Even though I have misophonia I am:

_____
_____
_____
_____

Cognitive Behavioral Therapy (CBT) for Misophonia

Example: Beliefs About Misophonia

Instructions: Complete the sentences to express your feelings and beliefs about misophonia, including what you would call it.

Misophonia makes me feel:

Misophonia makes me feel scared, angry, and like the world is out to get me. It also makes me feel tired, like I'm in pain, and like my world is shaking when I'm triggered.

If I didn't have misophonia I would:

If I didn't have misophonia I would work a job in an office or travel all the time. I'd go outside and be spontaneous and just live my life without planning every detail.

Even though I have misophonia I am:
A good friend, a good wife, and a good person. I give a lot of myself to others, and I am very creative, passionate, and a hard worker.

Cognitive Behavioral Therapy (CBT) for Misophonia

Worksheet: What is True About Misophonia?

Instructions: Reflect on what you believe is true and untrue about misophonia, both generally and when triggered, noting any differences.

1. **What is true about misophonia?**

   _____
   _____
   _____

2. **What is not true about misophonia?**

   _____
   _____
   _____

3. **What do I think is true about misophonia in the moment I am triggered?**

   _____
   _____
   _____

4. **Do I still believe the same thing when I am not triggered?**

   _____
   _____
   _____

5. **What is the difference between these two thoughts?**

   _____
   _____
   _____

Cognitive Behavioral Therapy (CBT) for Misophonia

Example: What is True About Misophonia?

Instructions: Reflect on what you believe is true and untrue about misophonia, both generally and when triggered, noting any differences.

1. **What is true about misophonia?**
   Misophonia is likely a neurophysiological disorder where certain sounds, called triggers, cause an intense emotional or physiological reaction. It's not a choice or a simple annoyance, but a real, involuntary condition that can significantly impact a person's life. The reactions can include feelings of anger, rage, anxiety, and disgust.

2. **What is not true about misophonia?**
   Misophonia is not a figment of a person's imagination or an attempt to seek attention. It's not about being overly sensitive, and it's not the same as being annoyed by a loud sound. It's not something a person can just get over or control with willpower alone. It's also not a fear of sound which instead is phonophobia.

3. **What do I think is true about misophonia in the moment I am triggered?**
   In the moment I am triggered, it feels as though the person making the sound is doing it on purpose to annoy me. The sound is the only thing I can focus on, and it feels overwhelmingly loud and malicious. I may think that this person is inconsiderate and rude, and my feelings of rage or

panic are justified and completely rational.

4. **Do I still believe the same thing when I am not triggered?**

   When I am not triggered, I recognize that the person making the sound was likely unaware of the impact it was having on me. I understand that the sound wasn't made with ill intent and that my reaction was due to my condition, not a personal failing of the other person. I am able to see the situation more logically and less emotionally.

5. **What is the difference between these two thoughts?**

   The difference is the presence of an emotional and neurophysiological fight flight freeze reaction versus a more measured cognitive reaction. When triggered, my thoughts are dominated by intense emotion, leading me to believe the other person is deliberately malicious. When calm, I can differentiate between the trigger sound and the person, understanding that the sound is the problem, not the person's intent. My non triggered perspective allows for more empathy and a more accurate assessment of the situation.

Worksheet: What Misophonia Means to Me

Instructions: Share your personal history and feelings related to your misophonia diagnosis and the term itself.

My first memory of misophonia is as follows:

_____
_____
_____
_____

What happened when I told others about misophonia?

_____
_____
_____
_____

How did you learn you have misophonia?

_____
_____
_____
_____

How did it feel learning that what I was experiencing is "misophonia"?

_____
_____
_____
_____

How do you feel about the term "misophonia"?

_____
_____
_____
_____

Does misophonia feel like it's a part of you or something that "does not fit" with your sense of self?

_____

_____

_____

_____

Example: What Misophonia Means to Me

Instructions: Share your personal history and feelings related to your misophonia diagnosis and the term itself.

My first memory of misophonia is as follows:

My first memory is from childhood, around age 8 or 9. I remember being at the dinner table with my family. My father's chewing and lip smacking sounds were overwhelmingly loud to me. I felt a surge of rage and panic, like I wanted to scream or run away. I had to leave the table, and my family was confused by my reaction. I felt immense shame and guilt for being so angry at something I knew wasn't a big deal to anyone else.

What happened when I told others about misophonia?

Before I had a name for it, telling people about my sensitivity to sounds was difficult and often met with disbelief. People would often say things like "Stop being so dramatic," "You're just overly sensitive," or "That's not a real thing." My frustrations were dismissed as a personality flaw. After learning the term "misophonia" and explaining it to a few close friends and family members, I received a mix of reactions. Some were immediately empathetic and understood better, while others were still skeptical.

How did you learn you have misophonia?

I learned about misophonia through an article I stumbled upon online. I was searching for "why do I get so angry at chewing sounds" and the term "misophonia" appeared. Reading the description of the condition was like reading a biography of my life. It described my exact symptoms and emotional reactions, which was a huge relief. The article also mentioned it was likely a neurophysiological condition, not a psychological or behavioral issue, which validated my feelings.

How did it feel learning that what I was experiencing is "misophonia"?

It was a powerful mix of relief and sadness. I felt an incredible sense of validation, realizing that what I was experiencing had a name and that I wasn't alone or "crazy." The sadness came from understanding that this was a real condition I had been struggling with for years, and it explained so many difficult situations and misunderstandings in my life. The name provided a framework to talk about my experience without feeling like I was making it up.

How do you feel about the term "misophonia"?

The term itself, "misophonia," which means "hatred of sound," feels inaccurate in a way. Sometimes I think people take it the wrong way and think it's just anger. However, it's a clinical term that helps legitimize the condition to others, distinguishing it from simple annoyance or general sensitivity. The term gives me a powerful tool to communicate my experience.

Does misophonia feel like it's a part of you or something that "does not fit" with your sense of self?

It feels like a part of me, but not in a positive way. It's an unwanted part of my neurobiology that I have to manage. It "fits" with my sense of self in that it has shaped my experiences and how I navigate the world—from where I choose to sit in a room to who I feel comfortable eating with. However, it's also something that feels foreign, an intrusive force that takes over my emotions and prevents me from being the calm, patient person I want to be. It's a constant negotiation.

Cognitive Behavioral Therapy (CBT) for Misophonia

Worksheet: How Others Feel About Misophonia

Instructions: Think about how you believe others view your misophonia and reflect on what you believe others perceive.

How do I think others feel about the word misophonia?

_____
_____
_____
_____

Am I bothered by how others might perceive misophonia?

_____
_____
_____
_____

What is misophonia actually like—and how is that different from what others think?

_____
_____
_____
_____

Cognitive Behavioral Therapy (CBT) for Misophonia

Example: How Others Feel About Misophonia

Instructions: Think about how you believe others view your misophonia and reflect on what you believe others perceive.

How do I think others feel about the word misophonia?

I think most people don't know the word misophonia at all. When I've tried to explain it, I've had to say "sound sensitivity" or "hatred of sound" because the term itself is so unfamiliar. To those who do know it, they probably see it as a very specific, clinical term that describes something they've heard about but don't fully understand. It's often misunderstood as simply being "annoyed" by sounds, rather than the intense, involuntary emotional and physical response it actually is.

Am I bothered by how others might perceive misophonia?

Yes, I am bothered by how others might perceive misophonia, especially when their perception is inaccurate. It's frustrating when people think I'm just being difficult, dramatic, or intentionally rude because of a sound. I worry that they see me as a picky or overly sensitive person rather than someone who is genuinely struggling with a neurological condition. This can make me feel isolated and misunderstood, and it can also create anxiety around social situations.

What is misophonia actually like—and how is that different from what others think?

Misophonia is not just about being bothered by a sound; it's a profound, sometimes debilitating reaction. When I hear a trigger sound, it can feel like a physical assault. My heart races, my muscles tense, and I can experience an overwhelming sense of anger, anxiety, or panic. It's an involuntary fight or flight or freeze response. Others often perceive it as a choice, like I could "just get over it" or "ignore the sound." They might think I'm overreacting, but in reality I'm experiencing a real physiological and emotional distress that is out of my control.

Worksheet: Misophonia versus My Personality

Instructions: Explore how misophonia interacts with or differs from your core personality traits.

Write in each side of the brain traits you believe are part of your personality and on the other side traits that are part of misophonia.

My Personality   Misophonia

Example: Misophonia versus My Personality

Write in each side of the brain traits you believe are part of your personality and on the other side traits that are part of misophonia.

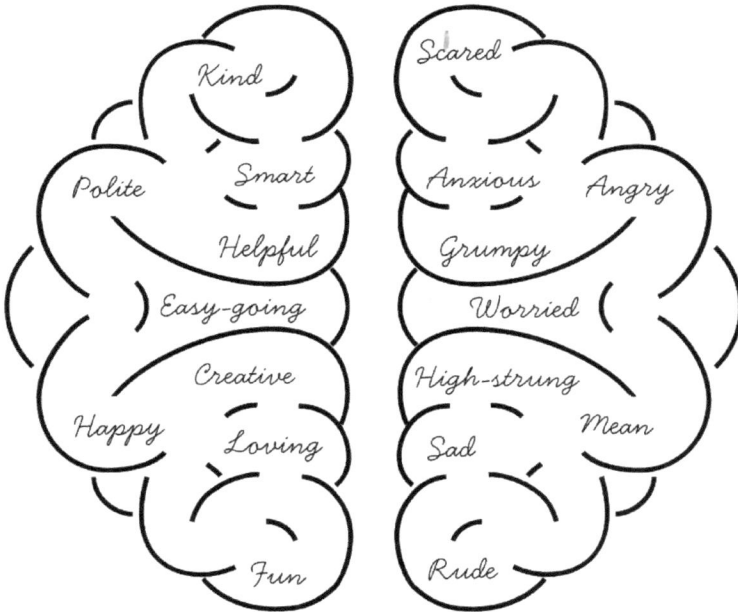

Kind, Polite, Smart, Helpful, Easy-going, Creative, Happy, Loving, Fun

Scared, Anxious, Angry, Grumpy, Worried, High-strung, Sad, Mean, Rude

My Personality   Misophonia

Cognitive Behavioral Therapy (CBT) for Misophonia

Worksheet: Misophonia and Daily Life

Instructions: Reflect on three ways that misophonia impacts your daily life.

What are three ways that misophonia impacts your daily life?

1. _____

2. _____

3. _____

Cognitive Behavioral Therapy (CBT) for Misophonia

Example: Misophonia and Daily Life

Instructions: Reflect on three ways that misophonia impacts your daily life.

1. *I can't enjoy things the way I want.*

2. *It adds strain to my relationships.*

3. *It makes my job harder than it should be.*

Worksheet: Misophonia and Me

Instructions: Reflect on how misophonia impacts your daily life and sense of self.

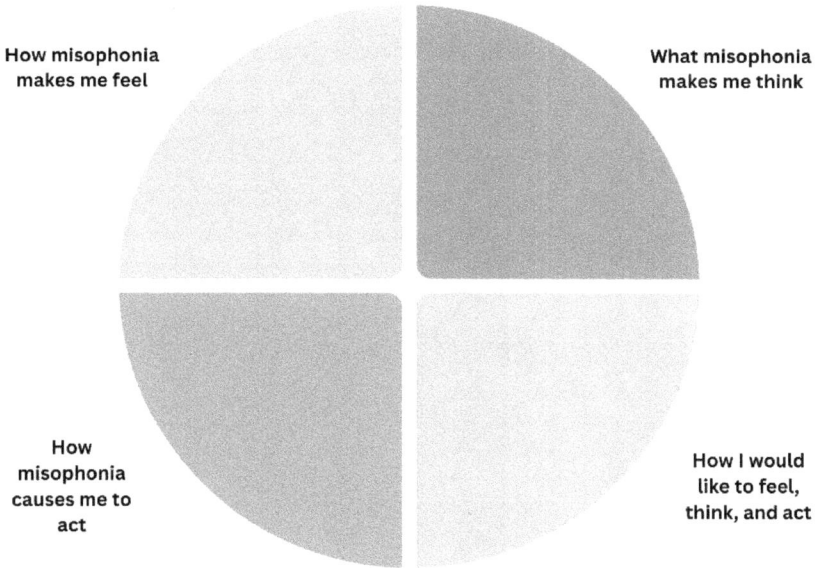

How misophonia makes me feel

What misophonia makes me think

How misophonia causes me to act

How I would like to feel, think, and act

Cognitive Behavioral Therapy (CBT) for Misophonia

Example: Misophonia and Me

Instructions: Reflect on how misophonia impacts your daily life and sense of self.

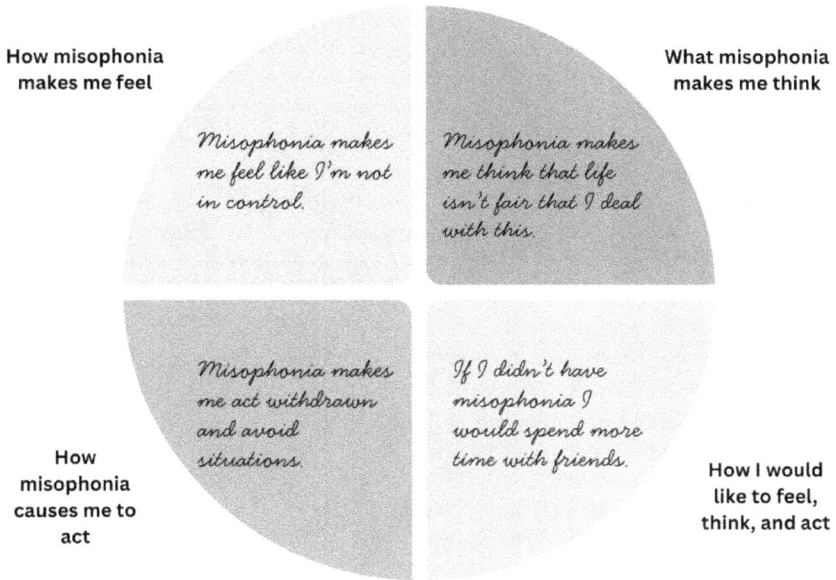

How misophonia makes me feel

Misophonia makes me feel like I'm not in control.

What misophonia makes me think

Misophonia makes me think that life isn't fair that I deal with this.

How misophonia causes me to act

Misophonia makes me act withdrawn and avoid situations.

How I would like to feel, think, and act

If I didn't have misophonia I would spend more time with friends.

Cognitive Behavioral Therapy (CBT) for Misophonia

Section 5: Misophonia Coping Skills

Before we discuss emotional and behavioral reactions to misophonia, I want to remind readers that while there are emotional and behavioral reactions *to misophonia,* the initial trigger moment of the fight-flight-freeze response is physiological. The exact moment of the misophonia trigger (response to stimuli) should not be considered an emotion or behavior through the CBT approach. Rather, we are looking at the emotional and behavioral reaction *after* the trigger has begun, and the individual is experiencing the emotional and cognitive aftermath. It is also possible that emotional and behavioral responses to misophonia happen outside the trigger environment, such as by avoiding potential triggers, finding adapting circumstances (for example, by only eating with music on), or maladaptive behaviors (for example, by shutting down without communicating needs).

Cognitive Behavioral Therapy (CBT) for Misophonia

Evaluating Coping Skills

While misophonia can often feel as though coping is impossible, it should be considered that individuals with misophonia are coping with the disorder regardless of their exposure to formalized coping skills specific to misophonia. Every person with misophonia, regardless of their age, has ways that they cope with misophonia. Whether these coping skills are adaptive or maladaptive is an important distinction to understand if coping skills are serving the individuals.

Part of coping with misophonia is beginning to understand the coping skills that are already present regardless of a prior understanding of them as being targeted coping skills. For example, if you listen to white noise or music or noise cancelling headphones, leave the room during trigger sounds, or even plug your ears during noxious sounds, you are coping.

Cognitive Behavioral Therapy (CBT) for Misophonia

Worksheet: How I Coped in the Past

Instructions: Describe past coping mechanisms, whether they helped, and alternative ways you could cope.

In the past I coped with misophonia by:

1. _____

2. _____

3. _____

This did/did not help because:

1. _____

2. _____

3. _____

How else could I cope?

1. _____

2. _____

3. _____

Cognitive Behavioral Therapy (CBT) for Misophonia

Example: How I Coped in the Past

Instructions: Describe past coping mechanisms, whether they helped, and alternative ways you could cope.

In the past I coped with misophonia by:
1. *Hiding in my room instead of spending time with my family.*
2. *Avoiding going to hang out with friends in case there are triggers.*
3. *Sleeping all weekend so I don't have to be overwhelmed.*

This did/did not help because:
1. *I started to feel lonely and like I wasn't close to my family so it made me sad.*
2. *Made me feel lonely and like I am a bad friend because I avoid my friends.*
3. *I feel bored and like I have no life because I spend most of my time avoiding others.*

How else could I cope?
1. *I could try spending time with family in small amounts so that I'm at least there sometimes.*
2. *I could spend time with friends one or two days a week but do a sensory activity first to keep calm.*
3. *I can find things to do that are less triggering so that I am not avoiding having fun.*

Cognitive Behavioral Therapy (CBT) for Misophonia

Assistive Devices for Misophonia

While assistive devices are not a primary feature of CBT, in the case of misophonia these tools can be beneficial and necessary for individuals dealing with the condition. CBT can also help individuals with misophonia who are not using their assistive devices due to cognitive factors such as embarrassment, worry of dependence, or a belief that they should not have to use such devices. Commonly I am told by clients that they know they *should* use assistive devices but for whatever reason they are not actually bringing them out of their coping skills toolkit.

In this chapter, I will mention assistive devices and tools that are commonly helpful for persons struggling with misophonia or sensory integration dysfunction; however, this list is not exhaustive and clinicians and persons with misophonia should be aware that these tools are highly specific to the individual. Many of these coping tools are based on an eclectic approach including sensory-regulation, mindfulness, narrative therapy, and more.

Assistive devices/tools for misophonia

- Earplugs
- Noise cancelling headphones or ear buds
- Stress balls
- Hand grippers
- Scents (essential oils, candles, etc.)
- Music player in room (Alexa, cd player, radio, etc)
- Weighted blankets, vests, and other weighted objects.
- Journal (to write down thoughts/triggers)
- Meditation apps or audiobooks
- Chewable bracelets, necklaces, etc.
- Fidget toys

It is my view that assistive devices for misophonia are an *adaptive* coping mechanism. Since misophonia is not a psychological phenomenon (Kumar, 2017), it is important to consider physiological ways to cope as well as tools to help the body self-regulate during these moments. Since sensory information is cumulative, I see no reason to limit these devices and frequently work with clients from a CBT perspective to encourage their use and tackle any personal thought patterns or behaviors that are preventing the use of these devices. The one caveat I have is that any devices that involve hearing (earbuds, earphones) should be set to safe listening levels to decrease the risk of hearing damage.

I have also found both with clients and in my own experience with misophonia that having access to numerous assistive devices and coping tools can lead to a decrease in anticipatory anxiety and an overall increase in quality of life in the moments when not triggered. Knowing that you have the *option* to use a device or accommodation is often a powerful tool in itself.

Cognitive Behavioral Therapy (CBT) for Misophonia

Worksheet: My Adaptive Tools for Misophonia

Instructions: List tools you've used for coping with misophonia either recently or in the past.

-
-
-
-
-
-
-
-
-
-
-
-
-
-
-
-

Cognitive Behavioral Therapy (CBT) for Misophonia

Example: My Adaptive Tools for Misophonia

Instructions: List tools you've used for coping with misophonia either recently or in the past.

- *Noise cancelling earbuds*
- *Earplugs*
- *Over the ear headphones*
- *Stress balls to hold when in a triggering moment*
- *White noise machines in the room*
- *Eye masks to block out light and help calm down*
- *Weighted blanket to help sleep better or keep calm while awake*
- *Candles or other scented items like wax melts or sprays in calming scents*

Cognitive Behavioral Therapy (CBT) for Misophonia

Worksheet: Using Adaptive Coping Tools

Instructions: For each trigger incident, record the date, scenario, coping strategy used, intensity before and after, what worked well, challenges, and lessons learned.

1. **What adaptive tools do you have or could get for coping with misophonia?**

   _____

   _____

   _____

2. **When do you use adaptive tools?**

   _____

   _____

   _____

3. **How often do you use adaptive tools?**

   _____

   _____

   _____

4. **Are there times you could use adaptive tools but do not? Why?**

   _____

   _____

   _____

5. **Could you implement adaptive tools more?**

   _____

   _____

6. **Do you think you overuse adaptive tools?**

   _____

   _____

7. **How do you feel when using adaptive tools?**

   _____

   _____

8. **Are your thoughts about adaptive tools true?**

   _____

   _____

9. **When should you use adaptive tools?**

   _____

   _____

Example: Using Adaptive Coping Tools

Instructions: For each trigger incident, record the date, scenario, coping strategy used, intensity before and after, what worked well, challenges, and lessons learned.

1. **What adaptive tools do you have or could get for coping with misophonia?**

   I have apple airpods, earplugs, and music and white noise apps on my phone I could use.

2. **When do you use adaptive tools?**

   I use adaptive tools when I am triggered or when I need to focus and can't be interrupted like while I focus on tasks.

3. **How often do you use adaptive tools?**

   I use my adaptive tools when I remember them.

4. **Are there times you could use adaptive tools but do not? Why?**

   Sometimes I don't use my ear buds because I don't want to seem rude or be accused of cheating if it's a test. Other times I just forget to bring them.

5. **Could you implement adaptive tools more?**
   I could probably make sure I have my ear buds with me just in case I need them.

6. **Do you think you overuse adaptive tools?**
   I think if I use them to try and drown out every noise I might not hear my friends or family, so that might be too often. But, I also think sometimes I need them.

7. **How do you feel when using adaptive tools?**
   When using my earbuds sometimes I feel like I should be stronger and not need them. I feel weak for not being able to act normally.

8. **Are your thoughts about adaptive tools true?**
   Thinking about it closely, I don't think it's true that I should be stronger, as I think it's okay to need help.

9. **When should you use adaptive tools?**
   I should use my ear buds whenever I am in distress or need to focus, but I should consider not putting them in until I need them so I won't miss out on important moments.

Managing Misophonia Triggers in the Home Environment

For individuals with misophonia, the presence of everyday sounds within the home can be a consistent source of discomfort. Auditory stimuli such as passing cars, lawnmowers, household appliances, or even footsteps may be perceived as challenging, thus presenting an ongoing issue. While relocating to a quieter setting might be considered an optimal solution, this option is often impractical for many due to financial, logistical, or tenancy considerations. Similarly, while structural soundproofing is often viewed as a definitive solution, it may not always be feasible or affordable.

This is where techniques such as sound absorption and sound masking become relevant. These methods do not necessitate major renovations but can still contribute significantly to reducing the impact of unwanted noise. By implementing practical adjustments to one's living environment, a calmer and less activating space can be cultivated. This chapter will explore functional, cost-effective strategies for sound absorption, sound masking, and minor soundproofing tips that can be readily applied throughout various areas of the home, including bedrooms, living rooms, and kitchens. Furthermore, the distinctions between soundproofing and sound absorption will be clarified, explaining their respective roles in noise management.

Understanding Sound Levels and Their Impact

Noise levels are quantified in decibels (dB), with the intensity of sound increasing logarithmically. This means that a 10 dB increase represents a sound perceived as approximately twice as loud. Understanding typical noise levels for different spaces can assist in evaluating whether the home's sound environment contributes to discomfort. General guidelines for residential noise levels include a quiet home environment at 30-40 dB (comparable to soft whispers or rustling leaves); living rooms and common areas at 40-50 dB (similar to moderate conversation or a refrigerator's hum); nighttime bedrooms at 30-40 dB (akin to a quiet library); and kitchens and bathrooms at 50-55 dB (typical of normal conversation).

Elevated noise levels can contribute to stress, sleep disturbances, and with prolonged exposure to potential hearing issues. The World Health Organization (WHO) advises nighttime noise levels below 40 dB to support healthy sleep, while sustained exposure to sounds above 70 dB may be associated with an increased risk of hearing-related issues.

Soundproofing versus Sound Absorption: Key Differences

Effective noise management requires an understanding of the differences between soundproofing and sound absorption. Soundproofing's objective is to prevent sound from entering or leaving a space. This is achieved by using dense, heavy materials to block sound transmission. Common materials include Mass Loaded Vinyl (MLV), soundproof drywall, acoustic caulk, and various types of insulation.

Sound absorption, conversely, aims to improve acoustics within a space by reducing echo, reverberation, and ambient background noise. This is accomplished through the use of porous, soft materials that absorb sound waves and convert sound energy into heat. Examples of common sound-absorbing materials include acoustic foam, fabric-wrapped panels, carpets, and curtains. While comprehensive soundproofing may not be accessible for all, sound absorption can effectively reduce noise levels and enhance comfort within an existing space.

What is Sound Masking?

Sound masking involves using background sounds to modify the perception of unwanted noise. Rather than eliminating noise entirely, it integrates disruptive sounds with consistent, low-level ambient noise, making them less prominent. Common types of sound masking include white noise, which covers a wide range of frequencies and resembles static; pink noise, a deeper, smoother variation of white noise that may support sleep and focus; and natural sounds, such as ocean waves, rain, or forest ambiences, which create a calming background.

Sound Masking Devices and Ideas

Several sound masking solutions can contribute to a more comfortable auditory environment at home. White noise machines emit a consistent sound that can mask sudden noises like traffic or distant conversations. Bluetooth speakers, when paired with ambient sound playlists, can provide calming nature sounds or white noise. Noise-canceling headphones utilize active noise cancellation (ANC) to reduce external noise. Fans or air purifiers can offer a steady hum that naturally masks background noise. Smart speakers can play sound masking applications or playlists on command. Additionally, tabletop noise machines offer customizable options such as pink noise, rain sounds, or fan noise.

Acoustic Panels: A Practical Approach to Sound Absorption

Acoustic panels function by absorbing sound waves to reduce echo and reverberation. They are generally straightforward to install and can contribute significantly to noise reduction, particularly in rooms with hard surfaces. Types of acoustic panels include fabric-wrapped panels, often suitable for offices, home theaters, and meeting rooms; foam acoustic panels, which are useful for home studios or gaming setups; polyester fiber panels, known for durability, eco-friendliness, and moisture resistance; perforated wood panels, which offer both sound absorption and a natural aesthetic; acoustic baffles and clouds, suspended panels that mitigate overhead noise; and bass traps, designed to absorb low-frequency sounds, reducing bass buildup in corners. Installation considerations include using removable adhesive strips for lightweight panels, opting for freestanding options like acoustic dividers or baffles, and choosing decorative panels that also serve as wall art.

Managing Your Sound Environment

While complete noise elimination may not always be achievable, practical steps can be taken to reduce its impact and enhance one's quality of life. Through the application of sound absorption, sound masking, or minor soundproofing adjustments, these solutions can help in creating a more peaceful home.

Misophonia Physiological Coping Tools

Since misophonia is impacting the nervous system (Kumar, 2017), it is no surprise that there is a physiological impact to misophonia. I often explain the impact of misophonia as follows—we only have one nervous system to manage all of the physiological impacts of daily life in addition to misophonia. Regardless of our coping skills or ability to understand misophonia, physiological symptoms can still compound and increase distress. Identifying physiological states can help a person with misophonia understand physiological states that can increase the severity of the misophonic moment.

- grounding
- progressive muscle reaction
- diaphragmatic breathing
- meditation
- mindfulness

Grounding techniques are designed to bring your focus back to the present moment and redirect your attention away from a trigger. When a misophonia trigger activates the nervous system, it can lead to a fight-or-flight-or-freeze response, causing you to feel overwhelmed and disconnected from your surroundings. Grounding helps interrupt this cycle by engaging your five senses. A common grounding technique is the 5-4-3-2-1 method, where you name five things you can see, four things you can feel, three things you can hear, two things you can smell, and one thing you can taste. This shifts your attention from the distressing sound to your immediate environment, helping to calm your nervous system.

Progressive Muscle Relaxation (PMR) is a technique that involves tensing and then relaxing different muscle groups in the body. The goal is to train your body to recognize and release muscle tension which is a common physiological symptom of misophonia. When a trigger is present, you may clench your jaw, tighten your shoulders, or tense other muscles without even realizing it. By systematically tensing and relaxing each muscle group (e.g., your hands, arms, neck, shoulders, and legs), you can learn to consciously reduce the physical stress response to a misophonic trigger, thereby calming your entire nervous system.

Diaphragmatic breathing, also known as deep belly breathing, is a powerful technique for calming the nervous system. When you are stressed or anxious due to a misophonic trigger, your breathing becomes shallow and rapid, which can worsen the fight-or-flight-or-freeze response. Diaphragmatic breathing involves taking slow, deep breaths that engage your diaphragm, slowing your heart rate and lowering your blood pressure. This technique can be practiced by placing one hand on your chest and the other hand on your stomach. As you inhale slowly through your nose, you should feel your belly rise, and as you exhale through your mouth, you should feel it fall. This controlled breathing directly signals your nervous system to relax.

Meditation and **mindfulness** are intertwined practices that cultivate awareness and a non-judgmental attitude towards your thoughts, feelings, and sensations. The goal is not to eliminate your misophonia but to change your relationship with it. Through mindfulness meditation, you learn to observe a misophonic trigger in a less aversive way (although you cannot remove the fight-flight-freeze response entirely). It is the cognitive after-thoughts we are changing through meditation and mindfulness.

While the above can be helpful for coping with misophonia, it is important to remember that the needs and wants of the individual are paramount for coping. If a person with misophonia is aversive to any of the above physiological coping skills, then they can be skipped entirely. The goal is not to cause more stress, but to adapt to the needs of the individual with misophonia.

Cognitive Behavioral Therapy (CBT) for Misophonia

Exercise: Grounding (5-4-3-2-1 Technique)

Instructions: The next time a misophonic trigger makes you feel overwhelmed, use this exercise to shift your focus back to the present moment and calm your nervous system.

See: Look around and name five things you can see right now.

Feel: Name four things you can physically feel.

Hear: Name three things you can hear (unrelated to the trigger).

Smell: Name two things you can smell.

Taste: Name one thing you can taste.

Exercise: Progressive Muscle Relaxation

Instructions: Find a comfortable spot to sit or lie down. Consciously tense each muscle group for 5 seconds, and then completely release the tension as you breathe out.

Hands and Arms: Make a tight fist, and then relax your fingers and let your hands hang loose.

Face: Squeeze your eyes shut and clench your jaw, and then release all the muscles in your face.

Shoulders and Neck: Hunch your shoulders towards your ears, and then let them drop.

Stomach and Chest: Take a deep breath and tighten your stomach muscles, and then exhale and relax.

Legs and Feet: Flex your feet, pulling your toes towards your body, and then release and let them fall.

Exercise: Diaphragmatic Breathing

Instructions: This exercise helps regulate your heart rate and calm your nervous system. Place one hand on your chest and the other hand on your stomach.

Inhale: Breathe in slowly through your nose for a count of four, feeling your stomach expand.

Hold: Hold your breath for a count of two.

Exhale: Breathe out slowly through your mouth for a count of six, feeling your stomach contract.

Repeat this cycle several times until you feel a sense of calm.

Cognitive Behavioral Therapy (CBT) for Misophonia

Exercise: Mindfulness and Meditation

Instructions: Find a quiet, comfortable space. Set a timer for 5 minutes. The goal is to observe, not react.

Observe: Acknowledge any misophonic sounds that arise. Silently say to yourself, "There is a sound," or "I'm hearing that sound again."

Notice Sensations: Pay attention to any physical sensations the sound causes in your body, like a clenched jaw or a tightening in your chest.

Let Go: Gently redirect your focus back to the simple act of breathing.

Repeat: When your mind wanders or you get caught up in a reaction, just notice it and calmly return your attention to your breath.

Cognitive Behavioral Therapy (CBT) for Misophonia

Worksheet: Physiological Checklist

Instructions: Answer each question to assess your current physiological state.

1. **Am I hungry?**

   _____

2. **Am I thirsty?**

   _____

3. **Am I tired?**

   _____

4. **Am I hot or cold?**

   _____

5. **Am I in pain?**

   _____

6. **Do I have a headache?**

   _____

7. **Am I stressed over something unrelated?**

   _____

8. **Am I in an environment I dislike or where I feel uncomfortable?**

   _____

Cognitive Behavioral Therapy (CBT) for Misophonia

Example: Physiological Checklist

Instructions: Answer each question to assess your current physiological state.

1. **Am I hungry?**

   Yes. I am hungry, I have not eaten yet today.

2. **Am I thirsty?**

   No, I am not thirsty.

3. **Am I tired?**

   Yes, I did not sleep well last night.

4. **Am I hot or cold?**

   No, I am fine.

5. **Am I in pain?**

   No, I am not.

6. **Do I have a headache?**

   No, I do not have a headache.

7. **Am I stressed over something unrelated?**

   Yes, I am stressed about work.

8. **Am I in an environment I dislike or where I feel uncomfortable?**

   Yes, I am uncomfortable because there is construction outside my window.

Cognitive Behavioral Therapy (CBT) for Misophonia

Calming the Nervous System

There are numerous ways to calm your nervous system, many of which involve breathing techniques, going into nature, soothing scents, and practicing meditation. However, there are also strategic sensory tools that can be incorporated. Occupational therapists use what is called a "Sensory Diet" to help with sensory regulation. The degree that these coping skills work for misophonia depends on the person utilizing them. The problem with calming the misophonic nervous system is that if you are still in the room with your trigger, each time you hear the sound you will be re-engaging the fight-flight-freeze process.

While this book will offer suggestions for calming the nervous system, it is offered with a caveat: if something does not work for you, or is not enough for the misophonic moment, this is not a failure. It is just an unfortunate part of misophonia that our nervous systems do not habituate to sounds (or visuals), and thus we do not *get used to them*. Because of this, the quickest easiest way to calm the nervous system is to remove the trigger.

With that in mind, I would suggest finding ways to accommodate misophonia that involve leaving the room, learning to ask people not to trigger you, utilizing devices like noise-cancelling headphones/earplugs, and negotiating accommodations in places that you cannot leave. For some therapists, this can seem counterintuitive as the initial response to *fear* in psychology is usually followed by the idea that you should *never feed the monster* and so you should learn to live in those moments. This, however, is a skill traditionally utilized for PTSD, OCD, and anxiety, rather than misophonia, which seems to have neurophysiological and not psychological underpinnings.

People with misophonia are exposed to their triggers daily—whether that is chewing, whistling, tapping, sneezing, or pen clicking. The sounds that cause a misophonic reaction are everywhere, and they are unavoidable. This is not a phobia where a specific stimulus can be avoided at length. For people with misophonia, the next trigger is always creeping around a corner. If exposure cured misophonia, we would all be misophonia-free!

Exercise: 4-7-8 Breathing Technique

Instructions: Follow the activity below to calm your nervous system.

In today's busy world, trigger sounds often feel unavoidable. Fortunately, there are simple techniques that can help calm the mind and body. One such method is the 4-7-8 breathing technique, developed by Dr. Andrew Weil and inspired by ancient yogic practices, this technique regulates the nervous system through controlled breath cycles.

How to Practice the 4-7-8 Breathing Technique

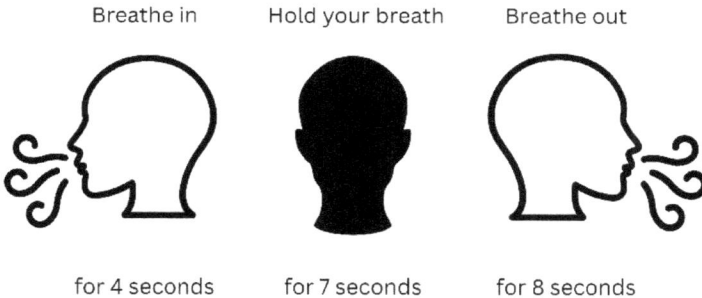

Breathe in	Hold your breath	Breathe out
for 4 seconds	for 7 seconds	for 8 seconds

The 4-7-8 breathing method follows these easy steps:

1. Inhale deeply through your nose for 4 seconds.
2. Hold your breath for 7 seconds.
3. Exhale slowly and fully through your mouth for 8 seconds.
4. Repeat as necessary.

This counts as one full cycle, and beginners are encouraged to repeat it up to four times. With consistent practice, many people experience noticeable relaxation after just a few rounds.

When to Use This Technique

The 4-7-8 breathing exercise can be practiced anytime you feel stressed, anxious, or overwhelmed, whether it is by misophonia or otherwise.

Misophonia Accommodations

Accommodations for misophonia are an important part of improving the quality of life for persons with misophonia. While some have theorized that accommodating misophonia may lead to a worsening of symptoms, I completely reject this hypothesis. As a person with misophonia myself, I have never found that accommodating my misophonia has made the condition worse—and in fact, accommodations are the reason why I am able to function in daily life.

I will relent that there is a degree of accommodation that becomes unhealthy—for example, completely disengaging with the world, avoiding individuals or events that are important to the person with misophonia, etc. Accommodations should focus on ways that the individual with misophonia can increase their quality of life and thus are adaptive coping mechanisms.

While accommodations are not primarily part of CBT, it is my belief that their use is paramount to coping with misophonia. Like assistive devices, persons with misophonia may be reluctant to accept accommodations due to cognitive and behavioral reasons. While accommodations are not CBT, they can be a useful tool for lowering overall distress and intolerance and lead to a lower threshold of sensory dysregulation. Rather than an approach that considers accommodations to be a maladaptive way of coping, I believe that accommodations should be used as much as possible to lower the overall distress caused by misophonia.

There is some limit to the amount of accommodation that should be provided for misophonia—but these limits are rather extreme. For example, if a person with misophonia is refusing to interact with loved ones, leave their room, or engage in important and meaningful engagements, then this becomes maladaptive and should be remedied. However, most people with misophonia are going about their day to day lives as best they can, and avoidance is *rarely* possible to an extreme level. Even those who live alone may be triggered by birds outside their window, pedestrians, going shopping, or other day to day interactions. I am opposed to cognitive models that consider accommodation to be maladaptive for misophonia—both from a clinical and personal perspective.

Sample Accommodation Letter

This sample accommodation letter is *not meant to be used as-is,* instead it is a reference tool for clinicians to use or for persons with misophonia to bring to their own clinician. This is not a replacement for your own clinical letter and is presented as-is for educational purposes. This letter was written for a client who struggles with misophonia in an office workplace environment.

Cognitive Behavioral Therapy (CBT) for Misophonia

Sample Accommodation Letter

To Whom It May Concern,

My name is [Clinician name] and I am [therapist license here]. I am writing this letter of support on behalf of [Client name] regarding possible accommodations which I believe would be helpful. While this letter is not a formal diagnosis, [Client name] has scored a 23 (moderate impairment) on the Duke Misophonia Questionnaire (DMQ). The DMQ is a validated scientific measure for determining clinical impairment for misophonia which is a lesser-known condition that causes a fight-flight-freeze response to otherwise normal stimuli (chewing, pen clicking, nail picking, throat clearing, and more). I believe that the following accommodations would be helpful for [Client name] based on our time together in a psychotherapy capacity:

- *Ability to leave long meetings.*
- *Ability to wear earphones/headphones when necessary.*
- *Ability to have a corner office or office with a door (while not always possible this would be the best case scenario).*

While I understand that some of these accommodations may not be possible, it is my belief that these adjustments would be beneficial for [Client name] and would not impede her ability to work productively but would rather help concentration and day to day functioning.

Thank you for your consideration.

Sincerely,
[Clinician name]

Cognitive Behavioral Therapy (CBT) for Misophonia

Worksheet: My Misophonia Accommodations

Instructions: Describe past accommodations, their effectiveness, potential future accommodations, and their feasibility.

1. **Have you ever had accommodations for misophonia?**

   _____

   _____

   _____

2. **If so, did they help?**

   _____

   _____

   _____

3. **What accommodations do you think could help?**

   _____

   _____

   _____

4. **Are these accommodations possible?**

   _____

   _____

   _____

Cognitive Behavioral Therapy (CBT) for Misophonia

Example: My Misophonia Accommodations

Instructions: Describe past accommodations, their effectiveness, potential future accommodations, and their feasibility.

1. **Have you ever had accommodations for misophonia?**

   Yes, I have had accommodations such as leaving a classroom, the ability to wear earbuds, and using quieter rooms for tests.

2. **If so, did they help?**

   Yes, the accommodations did help but there were still really hard times like even if I left there'd still be more triggers when I came back, I couldn't always have earbuds loud enough to balance blocking triggers and hearing, and sometimes even the smaller quieter rooms had a trigger in them.

3. **What accommodations do you think could help?**

   I think it could help if I had the ability to work from home most days so that I can recover more, but if I can't do that maybe it would be better if I could at least be the only one in the room for tests and maybe get somebody else's notes in case I miss important parts of class when leaving.

4. **Are these accommodations possible?**

I think these accommodations might be possible, it would be worth checking to see, and maybe if not there could be a compromise.

Planning Around Misophonia

While there are many parts of misophonia that individuals cannot control such as when and where they are triggered, it is nonetheless the case that planning to use accommodations, physiological coping tools, and assistive devices can make a world of difference. Depending on life circumstances and specific triggers, these plans can look different for each person with misophonia. Planning coping skills is one of the most powerful tools that persons with misophonia have at their disposal. While misophonia itself cannot be controlled, the ability to accommodate, use sensory skills, or have assistive devices are an invaluable way to improve the quality of life of individuals with misophonia.

Planning around misophonia can be as simple as ensuring that tools like earbuds, earphones, and stress balls are always carried by the individual with misophonia or as complex as a sensory diet planned with an occupational therapist or clinician. Sensory diets are planned activities that help the sensory system integrate and have traditionally been used in occupational therapy. For more information on sensory diets, you can reference *Misophonia Matters*, the prior volume by this author.

Cognitive Behavioral Therapy (CBT) for Misophonia

Scheduling Calming Your Nervous System

Create a weekly (or daily) calendar that includes things that may trigger you or that have triggered you in the past. Plan accordingly by scheduling calming activities before and/or after these potential triggers as much as possible. For the simplicity of this book, I have only used weekdays, but you can include all seven days of the week. You may also find it useful to use a calendar app on your phone or tablet rather than recording on paper.

Cognitive Behavioral Therapy (CBT) for Misophonia

Worksheet: Scheduling Your Coping Skills

Instructions: Plan and schedule specific times throughout your week to practice your coping skills.

Time	Monday	Tuesday	Wednesday	Thursday	Friday
7am					
8am					
9am					
10am					
11pm					
12pm					
1pm					
2pm					
3pm					
4pm					
5pm					
6pm					
7pm					
8pm					
9pm					
10pm					

Cognitive Behavioral Therapy (CBT) for Misophonia

Example: Scheduling Your Coping Skills

Time	Monday	Tuesday	Wednesday	Thursday	Friday
7am					
8am	Walk	Reading			
9am					
10am	Class	Class		Swimming	
11pm					
12pm				Dentist	
1pm					
2pm					
3pm					
4pm					
5pm	Calming music	Calming music	Calming music	Calming music	Calming music
6pm	Supper	Supper	Supper	Supper	Supper
7pm	Bath	Bath	Bath	Bath	Bath
8pm					
9pm					

Worksheet: Picking Activities You Enjoy

Instructions: List activities you enjoy that can serve as positive distractions or self-soothing techniques when dealing with misophonia.

Circle or put a check mark next to the activities which helped you feel calm or in a better mood in the past.

Meditation

Swimming

Swinging

Golfing

Basketball

Walking

Reading

Playing a game

Yoga

Baseball

Crafting hobbies

Lifting weights

Cognitive Behavioral Therapy (CBT) for Misophonia

Example: Picking Activities You Enjoy

Circle or put a check mark next to the activities which helped you feel calm or in a better mood in the past.

Meditation

Swimming

Swinging

Golfing

Basketball

Walking

Reading

Playing a game

Yoga

Baseball

Crafting hobbies

Lifting weights

Cognitive Behavioral Therapy (CBT) for Misophonia

Worksheet: Planning for Triggers

Instructions: Outline a plan for managing triggers by identifying coping tools, strategies for calmness, accommodation options, break plans, and self-talk.

1. **What tools can you bring to cope?**

   _____

   _____

2. **How can you remain "calm" before you're triggered?**

   _____

   _____

3. **Can you negotiate triggers, lessen them, or receive accommodation?**

   _____

   _____

4. **Can you make a plan for small breaks?**

   _____

   _____

5. **What would you like to tell yourself about being triggered (ahead of time)?**

   _____

   _____

Example: Planning for Triggers

Instructions: Outline a plan for managing triggers ahead of time.

1. **What tools can you bring to cope?**
   I can bring my earplugs and earphones with me to cope. I can also bring my phone and play a game that is relaxing to try and stay focused.

2. **How can you remain "calm" before you're triggered?**
   Before I'm triggered I can do something relaxing like going for a walk before going somewhere that is potentially triggering.

3. **Can you negotiate triggers, lessen them, or receive accommodation?**
   I think in some cases I can, like at the dentist I can have my mom wait in my place and text me when I am done.

4. **Can you make a plan for small breaks?**
   I won't always know when I can take breaks but I can think about things like going to the bathroom to calm down or outside for air.

5. **What would you like to tell yourself about being triggered (ahead of time)?**
   I want myself to know that even though this sucks right now, you'll get through this like you did before.

Cognitive Behavioral Therapy (CBT) for Misophonia

Coping with Unavoidable Triggers

When living with misophonia, it can be hard to accept moments where you truly cannot alleviate a sound or accommodate in the way you would prefer. For example, when living in an apartment complex or community area, you cannot control whether your neighbors are listening to music, have barking dogs, have lawnmowers, or have basketball hoops. This is something I have struggled with myself, and I empathize with persons with misophonia who are in this tough position. However, I believe that by *adjusting your expectations,* coping with uncontrollable triggers is possible. For situations such as classrooms, waiting rooms, or work, adjustments may need to be more controlled than those suggested for at home scenarios. In situations where there is no ability to leave, my approach is to go to the basics—earplugs, active noise cancelling earbuds, and leaving the room for breaks to reset the nervous system if possible. It is an unfortunate reality of misophonia that those specific moments will always be the hardest, but ensuring accommodations and tools are in place can help mitigate this distress.

Environmental triggers in the home can be particularly disorienting as one's sense of safety is compromised when triggered in the space where they are supposed to feel regulated. There can be bitterness related to this disruption of safety and anxiety about the trigger happening again since home is often the place we frequent the most. With that said, coping with this complex challenge requires cutting through the emotional moment of fight-flight-freeze and thinking in terms of "what can I do to cope" rather than "how can I make it stop?". In a perfect world, our triggers would no longer exist or at the very least no longer create a reaction, but that is not a plan for the moments where they *do* exist. The following exercise focuses on examining your particular triggering situation and thinking through ways to handle it. This can be repeated numerous times for numerous triggers or even employed regularly in the moment.

Worksheet: Adjusting Your Expectations

Instructions: Use this worksheet to work through how you will respond to a trigger that happens often. Repeat as necessary.

What is the trigger sound?

_____

_____

How often does the trigger sound happen?

_____

_____

How do I feel about having to accommodate myself at home?

_____

_____

Why is the sound unavoidable?

_____

_____

Am I able to leave the area where the trigger can be heard or do something else during this time?

_____

_____

If I cannot leave the room, what could I do instead?

_____

_____

Example: Adjusting Your Expectations

Instructions: Use this worksheet to work through how you will respond to a trigger that happens often. Repeat as necessary.

What is the trigger sound?

The trigger sound is basketballs being dribbled outside my window.

How often does the trigger sound happen?

The trigger sound seems to most often happen in the evening when my neighbors are home.

How do I feel about having to accommodate myself at home?

I don't like having to accommodate myself and I feel like I shouldn't have to adjust in my home. It makes me uncomfortable and I feel unwelcome.

Why is the sound unavoidable?

The sound is unavoidable because I cannot control my neighbors and they are allowed to play outside and utilize their yard just as I am.

Am I able to leave the area where the trigger can be heard or do something else during this time?

Yes, I can go to another room sometimes but other times I have to work as it can be heard in my office. Sometimes I go to the basement or my bedroom, or even take a nap so I can avoid that time of day but it's not always feasible.

If I cannot leave the room, what could I do instead?

I could use active noise cancelling headphones or earbuds during the time of the trigger since it's usually just for an hour or two.

Non-Negotiable Coping Skills

Coping with misophonia is not always easy and is often a challenge. Even somebody with numerous coping skills may find it hard to rely on their coping skills when in fight-flight-freeze mode, have other problems going on, or other health or life issues. However, it can be helpful to have coping skills that are non-negotiable and become the default for misophonia. By creating these non-negotiable defaults, the idea is that even in fight-flight-freeze mode these coping skills will become a habitual behavior. Non-negotiable coping skills should not be imposed on the misophonia sufferer by a therapist, family member, or partner. It is imperative that the misophonia sufferer has full consent over their coping skills and has decided that they will be using these skills regularly.

Of course, there is always a chance that these coping skills will not work continually or will require necessary adjustments. This should not be considered a failure but rather a part of the process. The idea is to have a set list of coping skills that are always available and at the top of mind. Preparing a misophonia go-bag for times outside the house and a printed list can be helpful to keep these skills at the top of mind. It can also be useful to print the list and post it on the wall in areas that are frequented.

For myself, I like to consider my "non-negotiable" coping skills as "being my own mom". For example, I would never let my child go hungry, be tired, continue doing a task when overwhelmed or burnt out, or locked in a house without going outside for air. Sometimes it can be hard to treat ourselves with the same amount of attention that we would offer for somebody in our care.

Worksheet: Non-Negotiable Coping Skills

Instructions: List your essential, non-negotiable coping skills for managing misophonia.

- _____
- _____
- _____
- _____
- _____
- _____
- _____
- _____
- _____
- _____
- _____
- _____
- _____
- _____
- _____
- _____

Cognitive Behavioral Therapy (CBT) for Misophonia

Example: Non-Negotiable Coping Skills

Instructions: List your essential, non-negotiable coping skills for managing misophonia.

- *Eating food if hungry*
- *Taking a nap if tired*
- *Going outside if cooped up*
- *Wearing noise cancelling ear buds rather than suffering through the sound and getting more upset*
- *Taking a bath when overwhelmed and needing to physiologically calm down*

Cognitive Behavioral Therapy (CBT) for Misophonia

Avoidance of Using Coping Mechanisms

The avoidance of using accommodations or assistive devices for misophonia is something that often arises in my clinical practice. Clients across different age groups have reported similar resistance to using coping mechanisms that have been suggested for misophonia. Sometimes this resistance is due to cognitive reasons, and other times there are physical reasons such as discomfort and headaches or another condition which limits mobility or accessibility.

Common reasons for not using misophonia accommodations and devices include, but are not limited to, the following:

- Belief that the people making the trigger sounds are justified in doing so.
- Resentment that accommodations and tools should not be necessary and are unfair.
- Discomfort with using devices such as earplugs and headphones due to physical reasons (dislike how they feel, head pressure, etc.).
- Physical disability (inability to go for walks, inability to easily change environments, etc.).
- Embarrassment or worry that others will judge the use of accommodations (if I wear headphones in class people will think I am weird).
- Worry about being perceived as being rude (if I wear earplugs my co-worker will think I am ignoring them).

While not every reason for avoiding accommodations is dictated by controllable factors, by focusing on views and beliefs that *can be changed*, there is room to increase adherence to coping mechanisms and thus lower the overall distress of misophonia. It is important to focus on what *can be changed* rather than what *cannot be.*

Worksheet: Remembering Coping Skills

Instructions: Create a list of reminders for adaptive coping tools and activities for misophonia.

- _____
- _____
- _____
- _____
- _____
- _____
- _____
- _____
- _____
- _____
- _____
- _____
- _____

Cognitive Behavioral Therapy (CBT) for Misophonia

Example: Remembering Coping Skills

Create a list of reminders for adaptive coping tools and activities for misophonia.

- *Make sure my earplugs or earphones are with me at all times.*
- *Remember to use my white noise machine.*
- *Take breaks when upset and do an activity that I enjoy that calms me down.*
- *Bring education with me if I am meeting a new teacher, clinician, or other person who may not know about misophonia.*
- *Be prepared to take time for myself after triggering moments.*

Section 6: Sustaining Progress

Since misophonia is a chronic condition without any known treatment that prevents relapse or alleviates all symptoms, sustaining progress is not necessarily a linear process. However, it is important for persons with misophonia to recognize their strides in the direction of coping and continuously review coping skills. While this book is written in the perspective of a 10-session therapy journey or a 10-week personal journey if the sufferer is using it as a workbook, that is not to say that further therapy would not be helpful for misophonia.

For example, an eclectic therapist such as myself may offer sessions for 'maintenance' of coping skills but may also move on to other prominent stressors that may or may not be related to misophonia. A primary example of this is if there is a conflict in a relationship, regardless of misophonia's involvement it is the case that couple's therapy or individual therapy may be considered. This program is meant to work in conjunction with other therapies and coping skills, rather than replace them entirely.

Cognitive Behavioral Therapy (CBT) for Misophonia

Worksheet: Coping Strategies Review

Instructions: List the coping skills you have tried, separating them into those you liked and those you disliked.

Coping Skills I Liked	Coping Skills I Disliked

Cognitive Behavioral Therapy (CBT) for Misophonia

Example: Coping Strategies Review

Instructions: List the coping skills you have tried, separating them into those you liked and those you disliked.

Coping Skills I Liked	Coping Skills I Disliked
• Earbuds • Earplugs • Leaving the room • Spending more time on exams • Sleeping more often • Talking nicely to others and explaining misophonia to try and limit triggers • Spending time alone when I need it	• Stress balls • Weighted blankets • Scents to try and calm down • Going for walks before triggers which just made me more anxious

Cognitive Behavioral Therapy (CBT) for Misophonia

Celebrating Successes

Misophonia can be an isolating and challenging condition. It is important to consider your successes and progress toward initiating coping skills within your life. Celebrating successes may feel difficult since misophonia is a condition that cannot currently be treated, but it is important to realize that every day we are doing things to help ourselves succeed and live with this condition. Like any other chronic illness, we should celebrate our ability to adapt and adjust to life with this condition.

Cognitive Behavioral Therapy (CBT) for Misophonia

Worksheet: Misophonia Successes

Instructions: Create a list of your successes since starting CBT-MISO.

-
-
-
-
-
-
-
-
-

Cognitive Behavioral Therapy (CBT) for Misophonia

Example: Misophonia Successes

Instructions: Create a list of your successes since starting CBT-MISO.

- *I went out to dinner at a restaurant and was able to stay the entire time without panicking.*

- *I spent 3 hours with family during Christmas dinner unlike my usual 30 minutes.*

- *Instead of breaking down I brought my earplugs and earphones and immediately used them when I needed to do so.*

- *I learned to explain misophonia to others and realized that people don't think I am crazy.*

Cognitive Behavioral Therapy (CBT) for Misophonia

Worksheet: Checking In

Instructions: Reflect on what was challenging due to misophonia, how you coped, what you could have done differently, and the differences in coping approaches.

What was hard today due to misophonia?

_____

_____

_____

What did I do to cope?

_____

_____

_____

What could I have done differently?

_____

_____

_____

What is the difference between how I coped and how I could cope differently?

_____

_____

_____

Example: Checking In

Instructions: Reflect on what was challenging due to misophonia, how you coped, what you could have done differently, and the differences in coping approaches.

What was hard today due to misophonia?

Today was super hard because I had to sit through a family dinner and my uncle was chewing with his mouth open. I could feel my body tense up and I just wanted to scream. It made me feel so frustrated and angry.

What did I do to cope?

I tried to use my headphones but my mom gave me a look that said "Don't you dare." So instead I just tried to focus on my own plate and eat as fast as I could. I was practically shoveling food in my mouth just to finish so I could get up and leave the table.

What could I have done differently?

I wish I had been more direct. Instead of just suffering in silence, I could have said something politely like "Hey, could you please try to chew with your mouth closed?" Or maybe I could have excused myself and gone to another room for a few minutes to reset.

What is the difference between how I coped and how I could cope differently?

The difference is that my coping was all about avoidance and internalizing the stress. I tried to mentally block out the sound and physically escape the situation as quickly as possible. The way I could have coped differently would have been more proactive and communicative. By either asking him to stop or removing myself from the situation in a more deliberate way, I would have been taking control of my environment instead of letting the sound control me.

Section 7: Conclusion

The purpose of this book is to provide a CBT-based approach to coping with misophonia (CBT-MISO). Coping skills are an ever-evolving world, and as we learn more about misophonia, skills may change or be adapted. At this point, coping with misophonia is about increasing quality of life as much as possible despite there being no official *treatment* that stops misophonia entirely. It is my hope that this book provides practical coping skills and CBT-based approaches for clinicians working with clients with misophonia and individual persons with misophonia looking for a self-help approach.

Clinicians and individuals looking for more information and coping skills for misophonia are encouraged to visit The International Misophonia Foundation website at misophoniafoundation.com. The IMF is actively looking for volunteers, researchers, and donors to help accomplish our goals of education, research, awareness, and coping skills for misophonia.

Cognitive Behavioral Therapy (CBT) for Misophonia

Misophonia Resources and Classes

Misophonia Coping Skills Coaching (Worldwide):
Coping skills for misophonia following the Misophonia
Matters perspective. Available worldwide as this is
coaching not therapy.
www.shaylynnraymond.com

Misophonia Therapy (Canada): Misophonia therapy
offered by Shaylynn Hayes-Raymond in Canada. Eligible
for insurance reimbursement. Only where eligible to
practice in Canada.
www.shaylynnraymond.com

Find coping skills classes virtually:
https://misophoniainternational.com/product-
category/classes/

Find clinician classes:
https://misophoniafoundation.com/courses/an-introduction-
to-misophonia-for-clinicians/

Misophonia International: Articles about misophonia
research, coping skills, education, advocacy, and more. Ran
by Shaylynn Hayes-Raymond
www.misophoniainternational.com

The International Misophonia Foundation: A 501 (c)(3)
non-profit in Columbia, Missouri. Offers education,
research, awareness on misophonia. Shaylynn Hayes-
Raymond is the director.
www.misophoniafoundation.com

References

The Bowen Center for the Study of the Family. (n.d.).
   https://www.thebowencenter.org/

Brout, J.J., Edelstein, M., Erfanian, M., Mannino, M.,
   Miller, L.J., Rouw, R., Kumar, S., & Rosenthal,
   M.Z. (2018). Investigating misophonia: A review of
   the empirical literature, clinical implications, and a
   research agenda. Frontiers in Neuroscience, 12(36).

Brout, J.J. (2021). A clinician's guide to understanding
   and managing misophonia from a self-
   regulation perspective: Regulate, reason, reassure.
   The International Misophonia Research Network.

Daniels, E. C., Rodriguez, A., & Zabelina, D. L. (2020).
   Severity of misophonia symptoms is associated with
   worse cognitive control when exposed to
   misophonia trigger sounds. *PLoS ONE, 15*(1).

Dozier, T. (2015). *Misophonia: The sounds that drive you
   crazy*. The Misophonia Institute.

Dunn, W. (2014). Sensory profile 2. Bloomington, MN,
   USA: Psych Corporation.

Fitzmaurice, G. (n.d.). *The Misophonia Activation Scale*.
   Misophonia-uk.org. Retrieved from
   http://www.misophonia-uk.org/the-misophonia-
   activation-scale.html

Jager, I.J., Vulink, N.C.C., Bergfeld, I.O., van Loon,
   A.J.J.M., & Denys, D.A.J.P. (2021). Cognitive
   behavioral therapy for misophonia: A randomized
   clinical trial. Depression and Anxiety, 38(7).

Jastreboff, M. M., & Jastreboff, P. J. (2001). Components of
   decreased sound tolerance: Hyperacusis,
   misophonia, phonophobia. ITHS Newsletter.

Johnson, S., & Dozier, T. (2013). *Misophonia and the Misophonia Treatment Protocol*. The Misophonia Institute.

Kumar, S., Tansley-Hancock, O., Sedley, W., Winston, J.S., Callaghan, M.F., Allen, M., Cope, T.E., Gander, P.E., Bamiou, D.E., & Griffiths, T.D. (2017). The brain basis for misophonia. Current Biology, 27(4).

Kumar, S., Dheerendra, P., Erfanian, M., Benzaquén, E., Sedley, W., Gander, P.E., Lad, M., Bamiou, D.E., & Griffiths, T.D. (2021). The motor basis for misophonia. Journal of Neuroscience, 41(26).

LeBouef, T., Yaker, Z., & Whited, L. (2023). Physiology, autonomic nervous system. StatPearls Publishing. https://www.ncbi.nlm.nih.gov/books/NBK538516/

Miller, L.J., Nielsen, D.M., Schoen, S.A., & Brett-Green, B.A. (2009). Perspectives on sensory processing disorder: A call for translational research. Frontiers in Integrative Neuroscience, 3(22).

Miller, L.J., Marco, E.J., Chu, R.C., & Camarata, S. (2021). Editorial: sensory processing across the lifespan: A 25-year initiative to understand neurophysiology, behaviors, and treatment effectiveness for sensory processing. Frontiers in Integrative Neuroscience, 15.

Moncrieff, J. (2018). Against the stream: Antidepressants are not antidepressants—An alternative approach to drug action and implications for the use of antidepressants. BJPsych Bulletin, 42(1).

Nesbit, S. (n.d). The sensory diet for adults and teens. Misophonia International.

Piccardi, E. S., & Gliga, T. (2022). Understanding sensory regulation in typical and atypical development: The case of sensory seeking. Developmental Review, 65.

Porcaro, C.K., Alavi, E., Gollery, T., & Danesh, A.A. (2019). Misophonia: Awareness and responsiveness among academics. Journal of Postsecondary Education and Disability, 32(2).

Remmert, N., Schmidt, K. M. B., Mussel, P., Hagel, M. L., & Eid, M. (2022). The Berlin Misophonia Questionnaire Revised (BMQ-R): Development and validation of a symptom-oriented diagnostical instrument for the measurement of misophonia. *PLOS ONE, 17*(6).

Rinaldi, L.J., Simner, J., Koursarou, S., & Ward, J. (2023). Autistic traits, emotion regulation, and sensory sensitivities in children and adults with misophonia. Journal of Autism and Developmental Disorders, 53(3).

Rosenthal, M.Z., Anand, D., Cassiello-Robbins, C., Williams, Z.J., Guetta, R.E., Trumbull, J., & Kelley, L.D. (2021). Development and initial validation of the duke misophonia questionnaire. Frontiers in Psychology, 12.

Rosenthal, M.Z., McMahon, K., Greenleaf, A.S., Cassiello-Robbins, C., Guetta, R., Trumbull, J., Anand, D., Frazer-Abel, E.S., & Kelley, L. (2022). Phenotyping misophonia: Psychiatric disorders and medical health correlates. Frontiers in Psychology, 13.

Schröder, A., Vulink, N., & Denys, D. (2013). Misophonia: Diagnostic criteria for a new psychiatric disorder. PLOS ONE, 8(1).

Schröder, A., Vulink, N., van Loon, A., & Denys, D. (2017). Cognitive behavioral therapy is effective in misophonia: An open trial. *Journal of Affective Disorders, 217*, 289–294.

Schröder, A., van Wingen, G., Eijsker, N., San Giorgi, R., Vulink, N.C., Turbyne, C., & Denys, D. (2019). Misophonia is associated with altered brain activity in the auditory cortex and salience network. Scientific Reports, 9(1).

Shanker, S., & Barker, T. (2016). Self-Reg: How to help your child (and you) break the stress cycle and successfully engage with life. Canada: Penguin Random House.

Siepsiak, M., Śliwerski, A., & Dragan, W. Ł. (2020). Development and Psychometric Properties of MisoQuest—A New Self-Report Questionnaire for Misophonia. *International Journal of Environmental Research and Public Health, 17*(5), 1797.

Ungvarsky, J. (2022). Bowenian family therapy. Salem Press Encyclopedia.

Waxenbaum, J.A., Reddy, V., & Varacallo, M. (2023). Anatomy, autonomic nervous system. StatPearls Publishing.

Woolley, M. G., Guetta, R. E., Rosenthal, M. Z., & Anand, D. (2025). Recognizing individual variability in misophonia. *Journal of Psychiatric Research, 184*, 232-240.

Shaylynn Hayes-Raymond

www.ingramcontent.com/pod-product-compliance
Lightning Source LLC
Chambersburg PA
CBHW062114020426
42335CB00013B/956